FIRST PEOPLES of NORTH AMERICA

THE PEOPLE AND CULTURE OF THE

BLACKFEET

KRIS RICKARD
RAYMOND BIAL

Cavendish
Square
New York

Published in 2017 by Cavendish Square Publishing, LLC
243 5th Avenue, Suite 136, New York, NY 10016

Cataloging-in-Publication Data

Names: Rickard, Kris A.
Title: The people and culture of the Blackfeet / Kris A. Rickard and Raymond Bial.
Description: New York : Cavendish Square, 2017. | Series: First peoples of North America |
Includes index.
Identifiers: ISBN 9781502622471 (library bound) | ISBN 9781502622488 (ebook)
Subjects: LCSH: Blackfeet Tribe of the Blackfeet Indian Reservation of Montana--History. |
Indians of North America--Great Plains--History.
Classification: LCC E99.S54 R513 2017 | DDC 978.004'97--dc23

Editorial Director: David McNamara
Editor: Kristen Susienka
Copy Editor: Rebecca Rohan
Associate Art Director: Amy Greenan
Production Coordinator: Karol Szymczuk
Photo Research: J8 Media

ACKNOWLEDGMENTS

This book would not have been possible without the generous help of many individuals and organizations that have dedicated themselves to honoring the customs of the Blackfeet.

We would like to thank in particular Cavendish Square Publishing and all who contributed to finding photos and other materials for publication. Finally, we would like to thank our families and friends for their encouragement and support along our writing journey.

CONTENTS

A young Blackfeet woman dances, wearing traditional clothing and bells.

AUTHORS' NOTE

At the dawn of the twentieth century, Native Americans were thought to be a vanishing race. However, despite four hundred years of warfare, deprivation, and disease, Native Americans have persevered. Countless thousands have lost their lives, but over the course of this century and the last, the populations of Native tribes have grown tremendously. Even as America's First People struggle to adapt to modern Western life, they have also kept the flame of their traditions alive—the languages, religions, stories, and the everyday ways of life. An exhilarating renaissance in Native American culture is now sweeping the continent from coast to coast.

The First Peoples of North America books depict the social and cultural life of the major nations, from the early history of Native peoples in North America to their present-day struggles for survival and dignity. Historical and contemporary photographs of traditional subjects, as well as period illustrations, are blended throughout each book so that readers may gain a sense of family life in a tipi, a hogan, a longhouse, or in houses today.

No single book can comprehensively portray the intricate and varied lifeways of an entire tribe, or nation. We only hope that young people will come away with a deeper appreciation for the rich tapestry of Native American culture—both then and now—and a keen desire to learn more about these first Americans.

In Blackfeet culture, it is customary to provide visitors with welcome bundles, such as this one.

*Life is not separate
from death. It only
looks that way.*

—Blackfoot saying

A CULTURE BEGINS

In the vast plains of the northern United States and southern Canada, the three tribes of the Blackfeet made their home. From the rivers, sprawling grasslands, mountain ranges, and rolling hills, they became one. A trinity of families, sewn together to create a sovereign nation. Little did they know how much they would need each other's strength to overcome harsh winters and an even harsher human climate. As settlers began their journey toward the west, this rich farmland full of bison, deer, bear, and other natural resources became a stronghold to be conquered.

Unlike some tribes, the Blackfeet were battered but never broken. Their spirits may have weakened in moments as they watched their children, brothers, mothers, fathers, and sisters die from smallpox or starvation. They never gave up and are a strong and resilient nation today.

The Creation of the Blackfeet

Known as the Lords of the Plains, the Blackfeet were a powerful confederacy of three independent tribes living in Montana and Alberta, Canada. With no written language, the people relied on stories to recall their origin. Whether about Napi, the creator of the universe, or other supernatural beings, these stories helped the Blackfeet to understand their history. Here is one story about how the land and the Blackfeet came to be:

> In the beginning, water covered the world. Napi and all the animals floated upon the water on a raft.
>
> Napi wanted to create land. He told the beaver to dive down into the water and to bring up a little mud. The beaver plunged into the water, but he could not reach the bottom. He returned to the surface, gasping for air. Then the loon tried, and after him the otter, but the water was too deep. Napi sent the muskrat down. The little brown rodent was gone for such a long time that

everyone thought he had drowned. At last the muskrat bobbed to the surface, exhausted and unconscious. The other animals pulled him onto the raft and noticed that there was a little mud on his paws.

Napi dried the mud and scattered it over the water. Each bit of mud grew into land. Napi stepped onto the land and gave it shape. He created valleys, through which rivers flowed, some tumbling into waterfalls. He formed towering mountains blanketed with stands of timber. He flattened the grassy prairies. He made berry bushes and plants, such as wild turnips and camas, whose roots and bulbs could be eaten.

He molded the buffalo and the other four-legged land animals that grazed on the prairies. However, the bighorn sheep could not walk easily there, so he took the bighorn sheep by its horns and led it to the mountains where it could dance among the rocky cliffs. While he was in the mountains, Napi created the antelope and turned it loose. But the antelope ran so swiftly that it fell and hurt itself on the jagged rocks. So Napi took the antelope to the prairies where it could race over the open land.

Napi then decided to create a woman and a child. He shaped some clay into two human figures and placed them on the ground. "You will be people," he said to the clay. He spread a robe over the figures and went away. In the morning, he returned and lifted the robe and noticed that the clay figures had changed a little. Every day, the figures had changed more, and on the fourth morning, Napi said to them, "Stand up and walk."

They walked to the river with him. They knew that he was their creator, and he told them his name was Napi. Over time, the woman had more children, and there were soon many people on earth who came to be known as the Blackfeet. Poor and hungry, these first people did not know how to obtain food for themselves. Napi told them how to dig roots and gather berries. He explained that they could eat small animals, such as squirrels and beavers. Napi also taught them how to make medicines from the leaves and roots of certain plants.

In those days, the buffalo had long horns with which they gored people, killing them. When Napi saw one of his children lying dead and partly eaten by a buffalo, he said to himself, "I have not made these people right. From now on, the people will eat the buffalo."

He went to the Blackfeet and asked them, "How is it that you do nothing about these animals?"

"We have no way to kill them," the people answered.

So Napi shaped a piece of wood into a bow and stretched a string across it. He cut straight tree shoots for arrow shafts and peeled the bark from them. Since he was master of all the birds, he caught one, took four feathers from its wings, and tied them to the shafts. But when he shot this arrow it did not hit the mark. So he tried using three feathers instead, and the arrow flew straight. Then he chipped some stones and found that black flint made the best points for the arrows.

Napi taught the Blackfeet how to hunt buffalo with the bows and arrows. He also showed them how to drive the herds over cliffs. He made stone knives that they could use to butcher the slain animals. The people then ventured onto the plains where they killed some buffalo.

As the people were cutting up the buffalo, Napi told them, "It is not healthy to eat raw meat. I will show you a better way."

He showed the people how to use a pointed wooden stick called a fire drill. Twirling the stick generated friction and heat that caused bits of dried wood, or tinder, to catch fire. The people could now cook their meat.

Napi also taught the people how to make buffalo hides into clothing and **tipis**. Over time, he showed the people how to make other useful weapons, tools, and household objects.

This is how Napi created the land and the people who lived there.

A Brief History of the Blackfeet

The Blackfeet have lived on the **Great Plains** of the United States and Canada for hundreds of years. Before 1850, they dominated the broad grasslands east of the Rocky Mountains. Their vast territory extended from the North Saskatchewan River in central Alberta, Canada, to the Missouri River in Montana. The Blackfeet—in their own language Siksikáwa, meaning "a person having black feet"—are made up of three tribes, or divisions, one of which is also called Blackfeet or Siksikáwa, or sometimes Siksika (SIK-suh-kuh). The other two divisions are the Pikuni, better known as the Piegan (pee-GANN; also spelled Peigan in Canada), and the Kainah, also known as the Blood. The origin of the tribal name is unknown. According to one tradition, ages ago the people lived in a different country where the dark soil stained their **moccasins**—or their moccasins might have been blackened by dyes or the ashes of prairie fires.

Of the three divisions, the Siksika live farthest north in what is now Canada, the Piegan are mostly in the south (in northwestern Montana), and the Blood live in the middle (around the South Saskatchewan River in southern Alberta). In this book, Blackfeet refers to the entire people, and the term Siksika refers to the northernmost division only. Closely allied politically, the three Blackfeet groups shared the same Algonquian language and are believed to have been the earliest Algonquian-speaking people to move onto the Great Plains. According to one theory, they lived in the woodlands around the Great Lakes before moving onto the plains well before the seventeenth century.

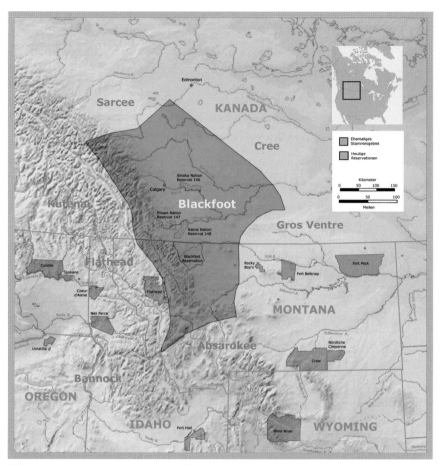

This map shows the original Blackfeet territory (green) and what territory remains today (orange).

They originally lived between the Bow and North Saskatchewan Rivers, but during the eighteenth century, they moved southward. Although they had no central chief, the Blackfeet formed strong alliances. Joining with the Gros Ventre and the Sarsi, the Blackfeet were often at war with other plains tribes, such as the Shoshone, Plains Cree, Flathead, and Assiniboine. By the middle of the nineteenth century, having defeated all their enemies, the Blackfeet had become the most powerful tribe on the northern plains.

The Blackfeet were hunters and gatherers who wandered the sprawling prairie in small bands, each led by its own chief. The bands followed the buffalo (officially called bison), camping in tipis near the herds. The buffalo provided much of their food, along with hides for making clothes and tipis. Before horses came to North America, the Blackfeet hunted buffalo on foot. They relied on dogs to carry bundles or pull a V-shaped carrier known as a **travois** (trav-OY).

During the early to mid-eighteenth century, the plains warriors acquired their first horses. The acquisition of horses quickly changed the Blackfeet way of life. The Blackfeet became skilled riders and horse trainers, traders, and thieves. Using horses as pack animals and mounts, they could travel more widely and more easily hunt the buffalo. They now had surplus meat, hides, and horns, which they traded with other tribes as far south as Mexico. Raiding the camps of other tribes for horses became a daring feat, especially for young men. In the dark or early dawn, warriors crept into an enemy camp, cut loose the finest horses, and quietly led them away while their owners slept.

David Thompson, a trader for the Hudson's Bay Company, journeyed into Blackfeet territory in 1787 and wrote the first detailed account of the tribe. During the early 1800s, American fur trappers also began to make their way onto Blackfeet land. Warriors killed a number of the trappers, whom they viewed as intruders. However, the Blackfeet soon agreed to trap the beavers and other fur-bearing animals themselves and bring the pelts to the trading posts. In exchange for the pelts, the Blackfeet obtained guns and ammunition, metal knives

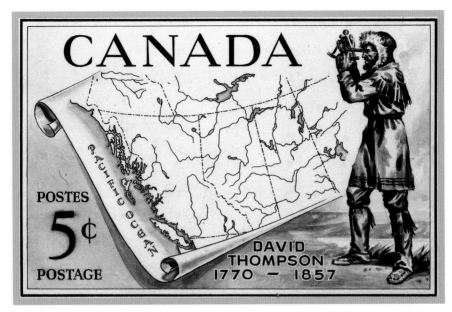

Explorer David Thompson is commemorated on this Canadian stamp.

and tools, glass beads, blankets, and other useful objects. However, after members of the Lewis and Clark expedition killed two warriors, the Blackfeet battled any American who entered their territory. Although they eventually resumed trade with the Americans, warriors occasionally attacked and destroyed the trading posts in their territory. Yet through most of the 1800s, the Blackfeet were engaged in the fur trade.

Contact with the newcomers had consequences. The traders brought smallpox, a disease against which the Blackfeet had little or no resistance. Devastating epidemics swept through the bands in 1781, 1837, 1845, and 1869. There were other conflicts. Settlers feared the Blackfeet, yet they wanted their land for cattle ranches and farms. In the ensuing years, the governments of the United States and Canada negotiated a series of **treaties** with the Blackfeet.

This painting by a Sioux member, not a member of the Blackfeet, illustrates the smallpox epidemic.

Not only were the Blackfeet forced to give up their territory, but their way of life was also gradually lost. Around the turn of the twentieth century, Western artist Charles Russell visited Montana and made several paintings of the Blackfeet. His portraits captured a vibrant people who were quickly vanishing from the northern plains.

When Blackfoot and Sioux Meet by Charles Russell

The People and Culture of the Blackfeet

Blackfeet territory had vast grassland, sweeping mountains, and buffalo.

Land and Culture

The homeland of the Blackfeet was a vast territory of grasslands, mountains, canyons, river valleys, and forests. There were also rugged, mysterious badlands and caverns, yet the predominant features were the broad, rolling plains and the immense sky. Some of the region became the state of Montana. This state is often called "Big Sky Country" because of the exhilarating sense of space. Blackfeet territory also falls into the Canadian provinces of Alberta and Saskatchewan.

The Blackfeet once ranged from the northern Great Plains of Edmonton and Calgary, Alberta, to the Yellowstone River in Montana. Bands occasionally roamed as far east as what is now the Montana and

North Dakota boundary, where the flat, unbroken plains gave way to craggy rock formations. The plains were dotted by isolated mountain ranges. At the western edge of their territory, the rolling plains were interrupted by the jagged, majestic peaks of the Rocky Mountains. The towering peaks were counterbalanced with breathtaking valleys cut by glaciers. To the south was Yellowstone country with many spectacular geysers blasting streams of hot water and steam high into the air. To the north, the plains unfolded for hundreds of miles before turning into a sprawling forest of conifers and the tundra of the arctic.

The winters in northwestern Montana and Alberta, Canada, were often very cold. As arctic winds blasted over the plains, temperatures plunged to forty degrees below zero—or lower. There were often blizzards that blinded travelers and buried tipis in deep snow. However, the climate could be mild at times, even in the winter. Unlike many areas of North America, where frigid temperatures settled in for months, the cold spells in Blackfeet territory were often broken by warm winds. Known as chinooks, these winds brought a few days of balmy, spring-like weather. The climate was also generally dry, with a yearly average of 15 inches (38.1 centimeters) of precipitation. The dry air meant that winters did not feel as cold or summers as oppressively hot as in other places. Daytime temperatures varied from an average of 28 degrees Fahrenheit (–2 degrees Celsius) in January to 85° (29°C) in July.

The terrain varied greatly in elevation. The highest point in Montana was Granite Peak in the Beartooth Mountains, which rose to 12,799 feet (3,901 meters).

At 1,800 feet (548.6 m), the lowest ground was in the northwest, where the Kootenai River flowed north out of Montana. To the west was the Continental Divide, which ran along the crests of the Rocky Mountains from Canada to Mexico. The Blackfeet and other tribes of the northern plains referred to the Continental Divide as the "backbone of the world." There, the waters of the North American continent separated, flowing westward to the Pacific Ocean or eastward into the Missouri River and other streams, and eventually to the Gulf of Mexico and the Atlantic Ocean. The headwaters of two of the great rivers of North America—the Missouri and the Columbia—were found in the nearby mountains.

The Blackfeet were primarily known as hunters and gatherers. The images captured in brushstrokes and photographs show their dedication to creating a life from the land and resources given to them. The riches they had in land, cattle, and bison were more valuable than human life to some.

Charles Russell's paintings allow the viewer to feel the Blackfeet's spirit. There are a number of prints depicting battles and hunting scenes. In the paintings depicting families with their horses, looking out over the plains, they each have a role and are looking in the same direction, with hope and determination.

The Sun Dance was very important to the Blackfeet culture. Here, a man participates in the dance by piercing his skin.

CHAPTER TWO

How can we plan our future when the Indian Bureau threatens to wipe us out as a race? It is like trying to cook a meal in your tipi when someone is standing outside trying to burn the tipi down.

—Earl Old Person, Blackfeet

BUILDING A CIVILIZATION

The Blackfeet lived a purposeful life. Each family, each person, played a very important role. Just like any society, there were leaders, warriors, peacekeepers, healers, and teachers. The tribes were families that borrowed strength from each other and created a way of life through ceremony and celebration. They continue this tradition to this day. They also had an astounding sense of equality, not only between men and women but also between classes. Perhaps that is why their **tribal councils** and government still stand strong today as a democracy that serves their people.

Equality and Societies

Each Blackfeet tribe was composed of bands of twenty or thirty families, or about two hundred people. Although the bands lived independently of each other, they considered themselves to be related. During the summer, they came together to hunt buffalo and hold ceremonies, notably the yearly **Sun Dance**. Throughout the spring, summer, and fall, they followed the buffalo herds. They also united in warfare. Each band had two leaders—a peace chief and a war chief. Chosen for his generosity, wisdom, and ability as a hunter and warrior, the peace chief managed the daily activities of the group. He was responsible for major decisions, such as when the band would move to another camp. He also acted as a judge in disputes. The war chief took charge when the band was fighting other tribes. Both chiefs served on a tribal council when the bands came together. This council selected a tribal chief to serve on a temporary basis. All decisions of the council were made by consensus, meaning that all of the members agreed on the action to be taken.

Men in the band were considered equal, although a man could achieve prestige based on his wealth, especially by the number of horses he owned. Blackfeet men were members of military societies, which they joined at the Sun Dance. In their late teens, several young men pooled their wealth to purchase membership in the Mosquitoes, the lowest of the men's societies. These young men chose a leader, who offered a pipe to the leader of the society. Each of the young men then gave pipes to the other members of the society. If these pipes were accepted, the young men offered horses and other valuable gifts in exchange for membership.

In 1833, there were seven men's societies, collectively known as the All Comrades. They ranged from the Mosquitoes, the youngest society, to the Buffalo Bulls, the oldest. Within the next two decades, the Buffalo Bulls ceased to exist because so many members had died in warfare and epidemics. However, the Blackfeet formed a new society of younger men called the Pigeons or Doves. Since society members lived in scattered bands, the societies were active only in the warm months when the bands came together to hunt. During this time, the peace chief asked one or two of the younger societies to police the camp and keep order in the buffalo hunts. At the annual Sun Dance, each society conducted its own unique ceremony.

Men and women could also belong to a number of religious and social societies, each of which had its own rites and rules. Among the Blood and the Siksika, women had their own exclusive society whose members were the wives of the most highly respected men in their tribes. The religious society called the Motoki built a ceremonial lodge similar to a buffalo corral before the annual Sun Dance. On the last day of the festival, they reenacted a buffalo drive into the corral. Wearing buffalo headdresses, some of the participants pretended to be the shaggy beasts.

The Sun Dance Lodge was an imporarnt building in the Blackfeet community.

During the winter, the bands drifted apart and settled in small camps. They lived on dried buffalo meat, roots, and berries. Trudging through the snow, the men hunted deer or elk. On long winter nights, people enjoyed singing, dancing, gambling, and an occasional smoke. They also listened to stories as the snows deepened around their tipis.

Housing

As the Blackfeet moved westward, they began to live in tipis. Relatively light and portable, these dwellings were ideally suited to their roving way of life. Made of wooden poles and sewn buffalo hides, tipis could be quickly set up or taken down. They could also be easily carried from one camp to another. The women simply lashed two of the long tipi poles to the shoulders of a dog or horse to make the travois, on which they piled the folded tipi covering and their household goods. With the ends of the poles dragging

The Blackfeet constructed their tipis themselves and painted the structure.

The People and Culture of the Blackfeet

on the ground, a travois worked even better than wheels on the rough ground of the plains.

To make the poles for a tipi frame, men cut down long, slender pine trees and peeled off the bark. The poles were dried in the sun, then dragged back to the camp. To build a tipi, women first lashed together the tops of four large poles and raised them, spreading out the bottom ends as they gradually stood the frame upright. Next they placed smaller poles in the gaps to complete the cone-shaped frame. The Blackfeet used about nineteen poles averaging 18 feet (5.5 m) in length. Some tipis had as many as twenty-three poles.

Making a tipi covering was a long and laborious process. Several women spread fresh buffalo hides on the ground and scraped away the fat and flesh with bone or antler blades. They allowed the hides to dry in the sun for a few days and then scraped off the shaggy brown hair. To soften the stiff leather, they soaked the hides in water for a few days, then rubbed in a mixture of animal fat, brains, and liver. Rinsing the hides in water, they worked them back and forth over a rawhide thong until they had become pliable. They smoked the softened hides over a fire until they were tan in color. Several women then laid out the hides, fitting them like puzzle pieces, and carefully stitched them together. Tipi coverings were usually made of twelve to fourteen buffalo hides, but as many as twenty could be used. A few larger tipis, having as many as thirty hides, testified to the owner's wealth. Before the introduction of horses, when dogs pulled travois, Blackfeet tipis were smaller, using as few as six buffalo hides.

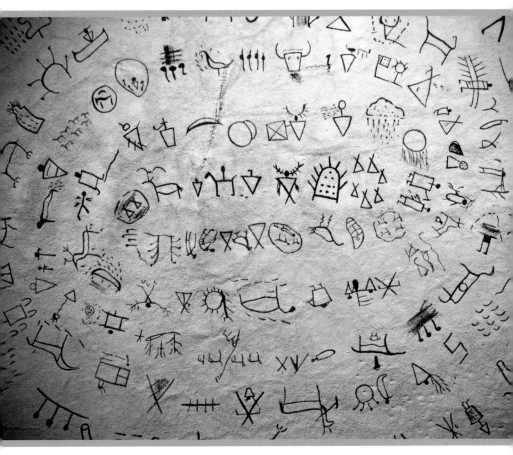

These symbols were written by the Blackfeet on buffalo hide.

To cover the tipi, the patchwork of hides was attached to a pole, raised to the top, and wrapped around the cone-shaped frame. Held together with wooden pins, the covering had two wing-shaped flaps at the top. When turned back, these flaps left a smoke hole. The flaps could be closed to keep out the rain, as could the flap covering the U-shaped doorway. The doorway always faced east, toward the rising sun. The men painted bold geometric designs and pictures of animals on the tipis. The designs not only related to key events, such as a victory in battle, but also reflected the complex beliefs related to **medicine bundles** and other sacred objects, rituals, and taboos associated with the tipi owner. According to origin stories, many tipi paintings were given to their first owners in dreams or visions.

A family of about eight people, including the grandparents, generally lived in a tipi. The few simple furnishings included buffalo robes and backrests. The backrests were made of willow sticks tied into a bunch with sinew and held up by a tripod. In the middle of the earthen floor, there was a cooking fire, the threads of smoke rising to the smoke hole. In hot weather, the Blackfeet raised the bottom edges of the tipi covering so the wind could blow through. During the winter, they banked the tipi with a berm, or sloped earthen wall, for insulation against the brutal cold. They also hung a buffalo hide dew cloth on the inside walls from about shoulder-height down to the damp ground. Decorated with paintings of battles, dreams, and visions, the dew cloth kept out moisture and formed a pocket of insulating air. With a fire burning and buffalo robes lining the walls, tipis stayed warm even during bitterly cold weather.

After the buffalo vanished from the prairies, the Blackfeet abandoned their tipis. They settled in log cabins on farms and ranches and no longer wandered the prairies. However, tipis are still a powerful symbol of their independent spirit at Sun Dances, powwows, and other gatherings. Painting tipis was once a deeply sacred expression of art and religion among most of the tribes living on the Great Plains. With the disappearance of the great buffalo herds in the late nineteenth century, people switched to canvas for tipi covers. The tradition of adorning tipis subsequently died out among most of the plains tribes—except the Blackfeet, who continue to paint vivid designs on their tipis.

The Importance of Horses

Originally, the Blackfeet had only sturdy dogs as work animals. Then, in the mid-eighteenth century, they acquired their first horses. The Blackfeet quickly came to depend on these swift, powerful animals. They not only rode the horses but also used them to carry packs and pull travois. Men occasionally caught mustangs from the wild herds that ranged throughout the American West, but they preferred to trade or steal horses that had already been broken. A man who owned many horses was considered to be quite wealthy, and giving horses away was highly respected among the Blackfeet.

The Blackfeet used superb, specially trained horses to hunt buffalo. These buffalo horses were taught to fearlessly gallop right alongside a stampeding bull. This enabled the rider to take aim with a bow and arrow at point-blank range. A good horse had to be strong and swift, with enough stamina to keep up with the thundering buffalo. It instinctively knew when to jump clear of the buffalo's dangerous horns. The horse had to be surefooted as it raced over the uneven ground. If it stumbled, the rider would be thrown under the pounding hooves of the runaway herd. A buffalo horse had to be agile and alert, instantly responding to the rider's wishes. With a bow and arrow in his hands, the rider could guide the horse only by shifting his weight.

Once introduced, horses became essential to the Blackfeet culture.

In a single buffalo hunt, the Blackfeet could obtain enough meat to feed the band for months. They also accumulated a wealth of hides and bones for making tipis and tools. Since they were often on the move, their household goods had to be light and durable. Pottery was often broken when taken to the next camp. The Blackfeet stored food, clothing, and other personal belongings in leather pouches called parfleches (par-FLESH-es). They carried water in animal skins and cooked meat and vegetables in a pot made from the lining of a buffalo stomach. If the buffalo herds continued to graze nearby, the band might camp in one spot for several weeks. But the Blackfeet usually followed the herds, pitching their tipis near streams and woods, where they had plenty of fresh water and wood for their fires. Often at war with other tribes, they usually camped at sites that could be readily defended against attack.

Blackfeet children became experienced with horses soon after they were born. When the band moved camp, mothers carried their babies on their backs as they rode on their favorite horses. As soon as children were old enough to sit up, they rode on a travois or in the saddle with their mothers. When they were about five years old, children learned to ride alone on a gentle horse. Tied to the saddle, they were taught to use the reins. At the age of seven or eight, children began competing in horse races with each other. When they were about ten years old, boys were entrusted with the care of the family horses—even of large herds. Before daybreak, the boys rose, went after the horses in their night pasture, and drove them to a nearby stream. After the horses had been watered, they pastured them near camp. During the day, they watched over the herd, taking them to be watered at midday—and again in the evening. At night they hobbled one or more of the horses to keep the herd from wandering too far from camp. When boys were twelve or thirteen, they tried their hand at breaking, or taming, horses. Sometimes, two boys led a horse into the shoulder-deep water of a stream or lake. One boy held the halter while the other climbed onto the horse's back. Then he quickly handed the halter to the rider. The horse bucked but soon tired in the water. The boy then rode the horse out of the water. If the horse was still too wild, it was led back into the water. Boys and young men also broke wild horses in marshes where the hooves bogged down in the mud. If the rider was thrown, the mud also softened his fall.

Purpose and Community

Not only did every person in the tribe have a purpose, but every resource they had served a purpose and kept them thriving in one way or another. The effect of necessity on the development of their culture was best exemplified by the importance of the horse to the Blackfeet. They were transportation to find a new dwelling while traveling across the enormous plains. They were utilized in the hunt for game and became important "family" members as well. Every part of the animals the Blackfeet hunted was utilized, too. The fat, bones, and hides became clothing, shelter, and ornaments.

Many Blackfeet women placed their young children into cradleboards, such as the one the woman here uses to hold her baby.

CHAPTER THREE

What is life? It is the flash of a firefly in the night. It is the breath of a buffalo in the wintertime. It is the little shadow which runs across the grass and loses itself in the sunset.

—Crowfoot,
Blackfeet Chief

LIFE IN THE BLACKFEET NATION

In order to understand the strengths and weaknesses of any culture, one merely needs to look at their family units. How well do they work together? How do they raise their young? What values are placed above all others? The Blackfeet are a strong people as they place a high value on family, equality, and loyal friendships. Though their innate trust was probably a weakness at times, it was also their strength. They understood the meaning of having a "battle buddy" both on and off the battlefield, and they understood the meaning of building everlasting friendships.

Life Cycle

The survival of the Blackfeet depended on families working together daily to provide themselves with food, clothing, and shelter. Traveling and camping in small bands for most of the year, the men hunted buffalo and other game. Women and children dug roots and picked ripe berries. Throughout the cycle of days and seasons, they marked the key events in their lives—birth, childhood, coming-of-age, marriage, and death. For each event, they observed many customs and rituals that had been passed down for generations.

Being Born

A pregnant woman wore a broad belt that could be loosened as she grew heavy with child. If she went into labor when the band was moving to another camp, she dropped out of the group and caught up a few days later with her newborn baby in her arms. If the band had made camp, the expectant mother retired to a tipi where she was helped by an elderly midwife. The old woman prepared a drink made of medicinal roots to ease labor pains. As she delivered her baby, the mother grasped one of the tipi poles for support.

The newborn was bathed and snugly wrapped in soft **buckskins** stuffed with a little moss for a diaper. A piece of the baby's umbilical cord was dried and kept in a beaded buckskin pouch to ensure good fortune. Boys had pouches shaped like a snake and girls had pouches shaped like a lizard. The Blackfeet believed that these animals enjoyed long, healthy lives.

A few days after the birth, the father called upon a respected man in the band to name the child. This was a great privilege because the Blackfeet believed that the name would deeply influence the child's life. Occasionally the child was named after a revered ancestor, or a name might be given in recognition of a brave or generous act of the father or the name giver.

The Blackfeet rarely used cradleboards. A woman usually carried her baby on her back. First, she swung the infant over her shoulders and then wrapped a robe or blanket around her body and that of the baby. Mothers typically nursed their babies until they could walk, sometimes until they were five or six years old. They believed that this practice would ensure that they would not become pregnant again until the first child was independent.

Growing Up

Children were encouraged to practice good manners and to obey adults. They were expected to sit quietly in the tipi while the adults talked around the fire. They were taught especially to honor the elderly. They had to undertake daily chores promptly and respect the medicine bundles of the family. Children were taught to accept good-natured teasing, but if attacked by a child of the same age, they were expected to fight back to the best of their ability.

Daughters learned how to perform household tasks and other duties by observing their mothers and grandmothers. Girls picked berries and did light

chores. As they grew older, they began to dig roots, carry firewood, and do other heavy work. Girls later learned to preserve food, prepare meals, dress hides, sew clothing, and make tipis. They also learned the art of decorating garments, parfleches, and other objects with porcupine quills, glass beads, and painted designs.

Boys were generally allowed more freedom than the girls. They learned about hunting and warfare from their fathers. They made small bows and arrows to kill rabbits and birds. Boys competed in rugged games and sports, demonstrating their strength and courage. Over time, they became good fighters and hunters. By their early teens, they were invited to participate in their first buffalo hunt.

Maturing

At the annual Sun Dance, mothers explained the virtue of fidelity to their daughters. Fathers pointed out the great warriors and reminded their sons of the Blackfeet adage, "It is better to die in battle than of old age or sickness."

Two boys of about the same age often formed a close relationship with each other and became best

The People and Culture of the Blackfeet

A Blackfeet warrior tells a young boy the importance of the peace pipe.

friends for life. As children, they played together. As they matured, they helped each other in courting girls, and then went to war together. If a man was wounded in battle, his friend risked his life to rescue him. He stayed behind until his partner could be safely carried away. The close friendship and mutual assistance continued throughout their lives.

Marrying

When a young man was able to provide for a family, he could take a wife. Once a young woman had mastered her duties, she was ready to be married. Marriages were often arranged by the parents of the bride when she was still a young child. Relatives and close friends also arranged marriages, but the man still had to convince the bride's father that he would be a good provider and a great warrior. Most men did not marry until the age of twenty-one, after they had proven themselves as hunters and fighters.

The wedding ritual centered on an exchange of gifts that included horses, household goods, and robes. After the wedding, the couple usually went to live in the tipi of the husband's family or in their own tipi. According to tradition, a man was supposed to avoid his mother-in-law, but a wife could speak to her father-in-law.

If a woman was lazy or unfaithful, her husband could divorce her. Similarly, if a man was cruel or neglectful, his wife could leave him. Because of casualties in war, there were more women in the tribe than men. Depending on his wealth, a man might have several wives. A woman's younger sisters, especially, might join her as co-wives of the one husband.

Two Blackfeet men sit and stand beside a burial platform.

Dying

At one time, the Blackfeet abandoned old and enfeebled people on the trail. However, after they

The People and Culture of the Blackfeet

acquired horses, they were able to carry the elderly on a travois if they were too weak to ride on horseback. If the head of a family knew he was about to die, he called his relatives together and explained how his horses and other property were to be divided.

Women prepared the body for burial. The deceased was dressed in ceremonial clothes. His face was painted, and he was wrapped in buffalo robes. The body was buried on a hilltop or in a deep ravine or placed on a platform of poles arranged in the branches of a tree. His best horse, outfitted with his finest saddle, was killed to aid his journey to the afterworld. Women and men mourned the death by cutting their hair, wearing old clothes, and smearing white clay on their faces. The women wailed and slashed their arms and legs, while the men briefly left the band.

It was believed that the spirits of the deceased journeyed to the Sand Hills, south of the Saskatchewan River. The spirits hunted and gathered there as they had during life. Invisible, the spirits often spoke with the living who passed through their territory.

Warring

Blackfeet men were among the best hunters, fighters, and raiders on the Great Plains—and they were often at war. Their principal weapons included 3-foot (0.9 m) bows, made of horn and backed with sinew, and arrows kept in otterskin quivers. They wielded stone war clubs and protected themselves with buffalo-hide shields. Warriors were honored for stealing a horse or taking a **scalp**, but they were most highly regarded for seizing a gun or weapons from the hands of an enemy.

Blackfeet warriors survey the landscape of Glacier National Park in Montana.

When going into battle or embarking on a raid, warriors called upon spiritual powers, known as war medicine, to bring them good fortune. Sometimes, a spirit appeared in a dream and shared its power with a young warrior. This spirit also told the warrior how

The People and Culture of the Blackfeet

to create a sacred symbol for the war medicine. Most often, an aged warrior bestowed upon a young warrior his own war medicine that had over the years protected him during many conflicts. The young man then took a pipe and other gifts to this seasoned warrior—often his own father or another relative. He prepared a **sweat lodge** for the older man, who prayed with him and shared some of his power with him. The symbols of this war medicine could be a war song, face paint, or a sacred object the veteran had once carried in battle. The symbols were often feathers or bunches of feathers worn in the hair, or they could be necklaces, headdresses, shirts, and knives.

The Blackfeet usually allied with the Gros Ventre and the Sarsi, and fought against most of the other tribes of the plains and plateau regions. Their principal enemies included the Flathead, Nez Perce, Kootenai, Assiniboine (after the nineteenth century), Shoshone, Crow, and Plains Cree. By the middle of the nineteenth century, the Blackfeet were at the height of their powers. Rival tribes and fur traders considered them the fiercest and most powerful warriors on the northwestern plains. The Blackfeet stormed eastward into Cree country and down the Missouri River past the mouth of the Milk River into Assiniboine territory. They raided southward to attack the Crow beyond the Yellowstone River. War parties ventured across the Rocky Mountains to sweep down on the Flathead, Pend d'Oreille, and Kootenai. The Blackfeet were especially hostile toward the Shoshone. Their attacks on this tribe persisted for over 125 years, until the Blackfeet drove the Shoshone back west over the Rocky Mountains.

Although the Blackfeet weakened their enemies by the attacks, their main purpose was not to destroy these tribes or seize their territory but to conduct raids. Hostilities most often took the form of raids carried out by many small parties. Each raiding party hastily came together and was disbanded as soon as the warriors arrived home. Killing and scalping enemies was not as important as capturing their horses. Young men needed many horses if they were going to marry and set up their own households. Risking their lives on these dangerous forays, young men became skilled warriors. The best raiders were not only courageous but also alert and clever fighters.

An experienced warrior led the raiding party. He was usually in his thirties, while those who joined him were in their teens or early twenties. The older man's good judgment and ability inspired confidence that the party would find the enemy camp, capture many horses, and safely return home. No one was forced to participate in a raid. The Blackfeet usually went on raids during the spring and summer, but they occasionally attacked neighboring tribes in the winter. In winter, less vigilant enemies were surprised by the raiders, whose tracks were quickly covered by falling snow. The night before they left, the raiders walked around camp, drumming on a piece of rawhide and singing their war songs. Friends and family donated food and supplies, such as extra moccasins, for the journey. Most parties were composed of twelve or fewer men, who gathered the next morning, well away from their camp.

To avoid alerting their foes with the rumbling of horses, the raiders usually walked to the enemy camp. They came lightly equipped with only a small pack containing extra moccasins, rawhide ropes for catching the horses, dried meat or **pemmican**, pipe and tobacco, and a medicine bundle. They also carried a bow and quiver of arrows or a rifle, along with a knife, which served as a weapon and a tool. With their sharp knives, the warriors not only butchered game but also silently killed enemies and lifted scalps. The men painted their bodies with the symbols of their war medicine. They waited to strike at daybreak while everyone was still asleep. As they approached the enemy camp, each warrior prayed to the sun or the moon. The leader and a few brave men slipped quietly into camp, throwing a little meat to the dogs if they barked. They sought the best horses, which were picketed by the tipis. If no one was awakened, they

Paul Kane's painting depicts a Blackfeet and a Plains Cree warrior battling.

would slice the rawhide tethers, lead the horses away, and return for more prize mounts. Meanwhile, the other warriors drove off the herd, which was usually pastured near the camp. The war party hoped to flee before anyone in the camp awoke and raised the alarm.

After the raid, the war party rode their stolen horses fast and hard for the first two or three days until they were some distance from the camp. They changed to fresh horses as soon as their mounts tired. If not pursued, they rested for a night and divided the horses the next morning before riding home. Pausing only to adorn their horses and paint their faces, they rode triumphantly into their camp, firing their guns in the air. The raiders gave away some of their horses to their family and friends. Each young man also gave a horse to the older man who had generously shared his war medicine.

Hunters and Gatherers

On the northern plains, food was usually abundant throughout the year. However, during winter blizzards and summer droughts, people went hungry and at times starved to death. The Blackfeet lived mostly on buffalo meat, although they frequently hunted other game as well, including deer, elk, bighorn sheep, mountain goats, and moose. Bold young men stalked grizzly bears for their claws, which they proudly wore as necklaces. Yet the Blackfeet were still wary of grizzlies, believing that they had great supernatural powers. Men also trapped beavers, otters, muskrats, and mink for their plush fur. Foxes and wolves were caught in baited pits or deadfalls. Weasels were especially prized for

Blackfeet thought grizzly bears had special powers so stayed away from them.

their white winter fur, used to decorate headdresses and ceremonial clothing.

The striking black-tipped feathers of the golden eagle were also greatly valued. The Blackfeet used these feathers to make **warbonnets** and decorate shields. They also caught ducks and other waterfowl and searched for their eggs, but they rarely ate fish or dogs.

The Blackfeet gathered wild fruits, nuts, and berries—especially serviceberries, chokecherries, and buffaloberries. In midsummer, women and children beat serviceberry bushes with sticks until the berries fell onto robes and blankets spread on the ground. In early autumn, they picked chokecherries and, after the first frost, they gathered buffaloberries from the thorny bushes. Berries were eaten fresh, cooked in soups and stews, or dried for the winter.

Using a birch wood stick with a sharpened, fire-hardened point, women also dug wild turnips, bitterroot, and camas roots. Wild turnips were eaten raw, roasted, boiled, or dried for the winter. Bitterroot was soaked in water and then boiled. Women baked camas bulbs in pits about 3 feet (0.9 m) deep. The pits were lined with flat stones, grass, and leaves, and then filled with the camas bulbs and covered with soil. A fire was kindled over the soil, and the sweet-tasting bulbs baked for about three days.

Camas flowers and bulbs helped make fires.

Like other tribes on the Great Plains, the Blackfeet hunted buffalo in various ways. Individual hunters occasionally stalked buffalo, but most often bands went on large communal hunts. Occasionally, men, women, and children worked together to stampede a herd and drive the terrified animals over a cliff. At times, groups of people surrounded small herds while

The People and Culture of the Blackfeet

Buffalo, formally called bison, roamed the plains and became essential to the Blackfeet way of life.

hunters shot the animals with bows and arrows. Once they acquired horses, the Blackfeet preferred to race after the herds, thrilling at the chase. When scouts had located the buffalo herd, the hunters approached from downwind. Then they got as close as they dared, the hunters switching from their everyday mounts to their buffalo horses. Galloping into the herd and eager to make the first kill, each hunter singled out a buffalo. Most hunters used bows and arrows because reloading a gun was slow and difficult, especially while on horseback. A hunter could also readily claim any buffalo killed by his uniquely marked arrows. Hunters favored short bows, no more than 3 feet (0.9 m) long, that could be easily handled. Slung over the hunter's back, the quiver held about twenty arrows with sharp

RECIPE
BUFFALO POT ROAST

In this basic recipe for pot roast, you may substitute beef if buffalo is not available. You may also wish to substitute other vegetables, but you will need a Crock-Pot or large, heavy cooking pot with a tight lid.

INGREDIENTS

4- or 5-pound buffalo roast

salt and pepper to taste

2 tablespoons flour

2 tablespoons cooking oil

½ teaspoon sugar

1 small onion, chopped

1 cup water or tomato juice

fresh parsley sprigs

8–10 small potatoes

8–10 small whole onions

8–10 fresh mushrooms

2 cloves garlic, chopped

2 carrots, sliced

2 stalks celery, chopped

Mix flour, salt, pepper, and sugar. Lightly pat the mixture on the roast. Heat the oil in the pot and brown the roast, along with the chopped onion.

Add water or tomato juice. Cover tightly and simmer on the stove top or in a Crock-Pot until the meat is tender (about 3 to 4 hours). Turn the meat occasionally, and add more water or tomato juice as necessary, but never have more than 1 inch of liquid in the pot.

Add vegetables and enough water to cover and simmer until they are tender (about 40 minutes). Remove meat and vegetables, and place on a serving platter.

If you would like to make gravy, add 3 or 4 tablespoons of flour and ½ teaspoon of sugar to the remaining liquid. Bring to a boil and stir until it forms a thick sauce. Add a little salt and pepper, if needed.

Slice the meat thinly across the grain. Garnish with parsley sprigs and serve with vegetables and gravy.

flint or iron points. Some men also hunted with short lances that they plunged into the heaving chests of the stampeding buffalo.

Afterward, the women skinned and butchered the buffalo scattered over the plains. Very little of the carcass was ever wasted. Each animal was quartered. The forequarters and hindquarters were then tied together with pieces of rawhide and slung over a packhorse. The fresh hide and slabs of back fat were thrown over the back of another horse. The ribs, hipbones, and neck were then tied onto the load. Wrapped in another bundle, the entrails were usually carried by the hunter's wife. Right after the hunt, people often ate some choice portions raw, especially the liver, kidney, and marrow from the leg bones.

Fresh buffalo meat was boiled in soups and stews or roasted. People savored boiled tongue and ribs roasted on hot coals on wooden spits. Women cleaned the small intestines, filled them with meat, and roasted them over the fire. The large intestine was also washed, filled with blood, tied like a sausage, and boiled. Women cut large amounts of meat into thin strips and hung them on racks to dry in the sun. The dried meat, stored in parfleches between layers of raw back fat, wild peppermint, and berries, helped sustain the Blackfeet when food was scarce. Dried meat was also pounded into small pieces and mixed with marrow to make pemmican. Sometimes, women added serviceberries or chokecherries for flavor. Stored in leather bags, pemmican was a vital, high-energy food, especially valued by warriors on long journeys.

The People and Culture of the Blackfeet

Clothes and Accessories

Women labored hard to tan animal hides and make soft, pliable buckskin to be sewn into clothing for their families. They also made leather moccasins, which they dyed dark brown, almost black. Girls and women wore long, one-piece dresses made of deerskin, goatskin, or sheepskin. Ankle-length and sleeveless, these garments were usually fringed, decorated with porcupine **quillwork**, and painted with geometric designs. Occasionally, they adorned their dresses with rows of elk teeth and leather pieces. In the winter, they put on buckskin leggings, attached sleeves to their dresses, and wrapped themselves in warm buffalo robes. Women also wore necklaces made of braided sweet grass and bracelets strung with elk or deer teeth.

Boys and men wore knee-length **breechcloths**, along with shirts, leggings, and moccasins. They wore buffalo robes in cold weather. Their knee-length shirts were left with the ragged edge of the deerskins but were fringed on the sleeves. Dyed nearly black, the shirts were adorned with quillwork, locks of hair, painted designs, and occasionally ermine skins. The designs represented a warrior's deeds of heroism. For example, a black tadpole shape meant that the warrior had been wounded in battle. Their robes were also decorated with painted designs and quillwork. Men often wore necklaces made of sweet grass and bear claws and teeth.

Women wore their hair loose or in two braids. For ceremonies, men wore their hair loose, but otherwise they wore a variety of styles. Some favored a topknot;

others had a bun in the back. Occasionally, they allowed a lock of hair to hang over their forehead to their nose. They plucked any facial hair. Men frequently painted their faces—black indicated a heroic act. They also painted stripes, circles, and dots on their faces in blue, red, yellow, black, and white. The Blackfeet put feathers in their hair, preferring owl feathers to the eagle feathers usually worn by the Sioux and other plains tribes.

During the winter, people wore fur caps of coyote, badger, or otter. The men occasionally wore buffalo-horn headdresses. Usually, they favored a warbonnet, having upright eagle feathers springing from a rawhide headband and strips of ermine fur hanging on the sides. This so-called straight-up headdress was originally part of the dress of the Buffalo Bulls society but was adopted by other warriors. The feathers stood up better in the wind, especially when riding on horseback, than the headdress of the Sioux and other plains tribes. The Blackfeet headdress also made a warrior a more visible target in battle, which showed bravery.

Tribal leaders and elders wore these distinctive headdresses until the early 1900s. However, the straight-up warbonnets were then replaced by the more popular Sioux and Crow headdresses, having eagle feathers extending over the back in what is called a shoulder-hang. It was believed that this type of headdress would be more recognizable when Blackfeet delegations traveled to Washington, DC, in the nineteenth century. In 1917, Glacier National Park and the Great Northern Railway in Montana required any Blackfeet working at the park's lodge to wear these

Blackfeet Chief Duck poses for a photo wearing his headdress and regalia.

headdresses. Orten Eagle Speaker, a headdress maker for more than forty years, explained, "The original Blackfeet headdress is the straight-up. In the Warrior Bonnet, a story was told for each real eagle feather. When the bonnet was full, if there were more stories or deeds, a trailer was added." These headdresses are still a source of pride for the Blackfeet. When **missionaries** and government authorities attempted to destroy Blackfeet traditional beliefs and practices, the straight-up headdresses were placed in the hands of ceremonial leaders. To this day, these sacred headdresses are carefully guarded.

A Blackfeet family dresses in "citizen's dress."

When the Blackfeet began to trade with Americans and Canadians, women came to use calico and other kinds of cloth in their garments. People continued to use buffalo robes for warmth and comfort, but when the herds vanished, they had to switch to Pendleton and Hudson's Bay blankets. Pressured by missionaries and the loss of the buffalo, the Blackfeet adopted what came to be known as "citizen's dress" at the end of the nineteenth century. Citizen's dress consisted of a shirt, pants, coat, and moccasins, which were preferred over stiff, factory-made shoes.

Women made many arts and crafts, sometimes from porcupine quills, such as were used here.

Arts and Crafts

The Blackfeet crafted practical objects for everyday use. These objects ranged from stones for pounding meat and seeds to fine porcupine or horsehair brushes bound with rawhide. The Blackfeet were renowned for the quality and beauty of their everyday objects, which included clothing, headdresses, tools, weapons, and tipis. Men painted tipis and other leather goods with stars and designs showing battle events. Women decorated clothing with quillwork or beadwork. The Blackfeet relied on the buffalo not only for its meat but also for its hides, horns, hooves, and bones. The Blackfeet made good use of virtually every part of the buffalo. They made more than sixty kinds of objects, including tipi covers, clothing, household utensils, tools, and weapons from materials supplied by the buffalo.

Stiff rawhide, in particular, had many uses. To make a parfleche, a woman scraped a piece of rawhide until it looked like white parchment. Then she folded it and stitched it together. Shaped like envelopes of various sizes, these pouches were usually painted with colorful designs. Rawhide was also made into belts and moccasin soles. It was stretched to cover drums and war shields. Most horse equipment—including bridles and saddles—was made of rawhide. Rawhide strips could be used as strings and straps for hobbling horses or rigging a travois. Rawhide could also be braided into tough ropes.

Women left the shaggy hair on the buffalo robes they tanned for winter clothing. They also tanned the hairless skins for use as tipi covers, clothing, and small pouches. Sinew was used as sewing thread and bowstrings. Men made tools—knives, scrapers, and needles—from the bones. Horns were softened and shaped into spoons, cups, and ladles. Strung on rawhide cords, the hooves made noisy rattles. Another kind of rattle, with pebbles inside, was made of rawhide stretched over a wooden framework and fitted with a wooden handle. Buffalo hair could be woven into rope halters and bridles. The shaggy hair could also be used as padding for saddles, stuffing for balls, and ornaments for tipis, clothing, and war clubs. Even the tail could be used as a flyswatter. For the Blackfeet, a single buffalo provided the materials for most of their tools and household objects. They even burned dried manure, or buffalo chips, as fuel for their fires.

Everything in the life of the Blackfeet had a purpose, including friendships, marriage, how they wore their

This photo shows a Blackfeet village of tipis in Glacier National Park, Montana, circa 1900.

hair, and their style of dress. They had a purpose for every part of an animal. They used them for food, shelter, tools, ceremonial instruments, and weapons. Nothing was wasted. One can clearly begin to see how they survived to the present day. The resourcefulness of their people and how they valued one another were, indeed, their two greatest strengths.

This drawing is of a Blackfeet medicine man, circa 1830.

CHAPTER FOUR

In the years since I began following the ways of my grandmothers, I have come to value the teachings, stories, and daily examples of living which they shared with me.

—Beverly Hungry Wolf

BELIEFS OF THE BLACKFEET

The symbol of strength in any belief is longevity. Faith should be something that is unwavering and provides a sense of continuing spiritual growth. The fact that many of the Blackfeet ceremonies and traditions are still practiced today shows how intrinsic they are to daily life for the Blackfeet. Again, their incorporation of both male and female in these rituals displays the tribes' sense of true equality.

There are few Western religions today that have that in their organization.

The Supernatural and Healing

Like other Native Americans, the Blackfeet believed in many supernatural beings, both good and evil. These spirits included the sun and the thunder and many animals. People believed that the land and all living creatures were blended spiritually with their everyday lives. They prayed throughout the day. Sweating served as a form of worship and a preparation for ceremonies. When the men gathered in the sweat lodge, they often smudged or smoked medicine bundles.

Young men went to remote places for solitary **vision quests**. In a vision quest, they sought guardian spirits who would guide them in their daily activities and in important endeavors, such as going to war or hunting buffalo. Guardian spirits—often in the form of animals—brought good fortune and taught important skills. In the vision, the spirits revealed songs, rituals, and powerful objects known as **talismans**. The youth gathered these talismans and placed them in a medicine bundle. During social and religious ceremonies, he drew upon the power of the medicine bundle, as well as the songs and rituals. Men who had received a vision that might benefit the entire tribe became holy men. It was believed that their medicine bundles were especially strong. Individuals, societies, and bands all owned medicine bundles, which included sacred pipes. The most powerful medicine bundle was the beaver medicine bundle, used to charm the buffalo by a group known as the Beaver Men. This bundle

Feathers were important to the Blackfeet.

also aided in planting sacred tobacco, which was used in rituals, notably the medicine pipe ceremony. Medicine bundles ensured a long and prosperous life. Considered quite valuable, the medicine bundles were traded among tribal members in elaborate ceremonies.

Shamans, or medicine men, were responsible for curing illnesses and healing injuries. There were a number of medicine women among the Blackfeet who, like the men, had acquired their ability to heal the sick through a vision. The Blackfeet believed that illnesses were caused by the presence of an evil spirit

Here, a Blackfeet man named Big Springs prays to the sun.

The People and Culture of the Blackfeet

in the body. The shaman undertook rituals in which the good spirits were asked to drive away the evil spirits. They often removed an object from the sick person as proof that the ritual had worked. Shamans also treated injuries, such as cuts, with medicinal herbs. They learned about these medicines by serving an apprenticeship with an experienced healer. Horses were usually offered as payment for the services of a shaman.

Rituals and Celebrations

The most important ceremony was the Sun Dance, held in midsummer in a special lodge. The Sun Dance was most likely adopted from the Arapaho or the Gros Ventre in the mid-eighteenth century. Unlike the other tribes on the Great Plains, Blackfeet women also took part in the Sun Dance. In particular, the medicine woman was a key figure whose virtue and preparations influenced the success of the sacred event.

The Sun Dance lodge was built of cottonwood around a tall center pole, and the dance began. Over the course of four days, the dancers, who had taken sacred vows, fasted and drank no water. Through reverent songs, they called upon the sun to bring them strength and good fortune. Some dancers pierced the muscles of their chests with sticks attached with rawhide thongs to the center pole. The dancers then pulled away from the pole until the sticks were torn loose. Other men and women cut off fingers or dug chunks of flesh from the arms and legs. Although the United States and Canadian governments outlawed the Sun Dance in the late nineteenth century, it never

In 1872, Heart Butte Day School became the first public day school for Blackfeet children.

vanished, and many Blackfeet continue to take part in this sacred event.

In the early 1800s, missionaries arrived in Montana, but the Blackfeet resisted the missionaries' efforts to convert them to Christianity. In the late 1800s, mission schools were opened for the tribe. Gradually, traditional beliefs were undermined, and many people converted. Although the Blackfeet continue to belong to secret societies and practice the Sun Dance, many are also Christians.

Fun and Games

The Blackfeet enjoyed a wide variety of sports, games, and amusing pastimes. They often kidded each other and told humorous stories. In campfire yarns, the creator Napi became a trickster who took advantage

The Blackfeet created paintings on many objects, including shields.

of just about everyone—though in the most amusing stories his tricks backfired, and he became the dupe.

Children played with toys. In the winter, boys spun tops on packed snow or river ice. Lashing together a log and tree limbs and attaching horsehair for mane and tail, men cleverly fashioned hobbyhorses on which young children practiced their riding skills. Children also enjoyed hide-and-seek, swimming in the summer, and sledding in the winter. Much of their play imitated adult activities, and they often played house. Boys snared gophers and dried their skins, which girls then sewed into miniature tipi covers. With sticks and skins, girls also made tiny travois and parfleches. Girls played with dolls made by their mothers and grandmothers, and practiced housekeeping, handicrafts, and moving camp.

Girls sometimes played a game similar to crack-the-whip. Seven or eight girls formed a line, each holding onto the waist of the girl in front of her. Singing "skunk with no hair on the backbone," the leader walked, then began to run, trying to swing the line so that she could touch the last girl. If the girl was tagged, she became the leader and the girl in front became the last in line. The boys enjoyed vigorous contests, such as wrestling, archery, and spear throwing. These activities toughened their bodies and enhanced the skills that would be useful in hunting and warfare. To mimic a buffalo hunt, one boy dragged a chunk of meat on a rawhide rope while the other boys took aim with bows and arrows. Sometimes, he stopped and swung the meat over his head as the boys shot at it. Boys also hunted small game—rabbits in winter and gophers in early summer. They took baby hawks from their nests and raised them in cages made of woven willow branches. By the following spring, they had hawk feathers for fletching their arrows. Boys also competed in the clay war game. In this game, two teams went to the riverbank and cut willow branches. Using the springy willow branches, they shot balls of wet clay at each other.

As they became teenagers, boys and girls enjoyed a hockey game known as batting ours. Swinging curved sticks of cherry wood, teams of ten to fifteen people competed to knock a hair-stuffed, skin-covered ball through a goal. The goals, consisting of two poles placed 4 feet (1.2 m) apart, were located about 100 yards (91 m) apart, at opposite ends of the playing field. In this tough, fast-paced game, teams often battled for hours before a goal was scored. Older girls also played the less strenuous Cree Women's game, in which players formed a circle and batted a large hair-stuffed ball. The object was to keep the ball up in the air.

Adult women enjoyed a kind of dice game known as the travois game. Two women sat opposite each other with five pieces of buffalo bones between them. The pieces were about 6 inches (15 cm) long and 0.75 inches (1.9 cm) wide, tapering at the ends. Four of the pieces were "snakes" marked with wavy lines, and the fifth had bands near each end. One player cast the four snake pieces from a bone cup, trying to turn them all "snake side" up. If she did so, she won the game, but this rarely occurred. She then had eight chances to turn over the plain-side pieces by throwing the fifth piece at them like a spear. A count was taken of the snake-side-up pieces, and then the opponent had her turn. When one player gained the previously agreed-upon number of points, she was declared the winner. Men often gathered when skilled players were engaged in a hotly contested match. They eagerly bet horses, weapons, buffalo robes, and other valuables on their favorite player.

Two or more women played a similar game in which they tossed small wooden pieces, each marked like dice. They placed the dice in a wooden bowl and tossed them in the air, counting the marks on the turned-up sides. They passed the bowl and dice around the group until one player had gained a certain number of points. Men played and gambled heavily on a guessing game known as fancy gambling. The game was played with two small bone cylinders, one of which was wrapped with a narrow band of rawhide. Two teams sat opposite each other with a pole between them. While his team members sang and beat the pole with wooden clubs, one contestant quickly passed the bones in his hands, then hid them in his clenched fists. An opposing player then had to guess which hand held the marked bone. Twelve willow sticks were used as counters, and the team that gained them all won the game. Both the players and the onlookers bet heavily on these games, and some unlucky gamblers lost everything they owned—even the clothes on their backs.

One of the men's societies' favorite sports was the wheel game, also known as the hoop-and-pole game. One society challenged another by sending tobacco to its leader. The hoop was about 3 inches (7.6 cm) in diameter. It was made of the neck cord of a buffalo and had a center hole, or bull's-eye, and spokes of rawhide cord strung with colored beads. Contestants prayed and recounted their heroics in battle. The hoop was then rolled on smooth ground and team members threw small spears, trying to hit the bull's-eye or score points by striking the beads. Young men played the

Young Blackfeet men would often participate in horse races.

game as a means of gambling. Boys played a similar kind of hoop-and-pole game with a larger target. The Blackfeet believe that Napi once played the hoop-and-pole game against a Kootenai man for high stakes—the control of the buffalo herds. Napi won the match, which is why there were never any buffalo west of the Rockies.

The most exciting competitions were foot and horse races. Clad only in breechcloth and moccasins, boys and young men ran courses of 0.5 miles (0.8 kilometers) or longer. The swiftest runners were proud of themselves and admired by others in the societies and bands. When everyone gathered in camp during the summer, horse races were especially thrilling events. Societies challenged each other and raced their best horses on courses from 2 to 4 miles (3.2 to 6.4 km) long. The horses were closely watched before the race, judges were stationed at the finish line, and people often made extravagant bets. After the race, the winners joyfully claimed the horses and other valuables that had been wagered. Members of the losing society often planned a raid to steal a fast horse and recover the property they had lost.

On summer nights, people enjoyed social dancing to the rhythmic beat of the drums. During long winter evenings, they listened to stories about the origin of sacred rituals, courageous acts of proud warriors, and the adventures of clever Napi. Here is one story about Napi's search for the buffalo:

> Long ago, the people were very hungry. No
> buffalo or antelope could be found on the

prairie. Grass grew on the trails once used by the elk and deer. There were not even rabbits in the bushes. The people prayed, "Napi, help us now or we will surely die. It is useless to kindle a fire. We cannot use our bows and arrows. Our knives remain in their sheaths."

Hearing them, Napi went out in search of food. He was accompanied by a young man, who was the son of a chief. For many days, they journeyed over the prairies, but they did not see any animals. They survived on roots and berries. One day they climbed to the top of a high ridge and gazed over the land. Far away, they noticed a solitary lodge by a stream.

"Who can be there, camping alone, far from any friends?" asked the young man.

"It is he who has hidden all the animals from the people," said Napi. "He has a wife and a little boy."

As they went down to the lodge, Napi told the young man that they would disguise themselves. Napi then changed himself into a small dog. "It is I," he said. The young man then transformed himself into a wooden stick for digging roots and said, "It is I."

The little boy quickly spotted the dog and he eagerly brought it to the lodge. He said to his father, "See, what a pretty dog I have found."

"That is no dog," his father said. "Get rid of it."

The little boy cried, but his father made him take the dog out of the lodge. The boy then came upon the root digger. Picking up the dog and the digging stick, he brought them into the lodge. "Look, Mother," he said. "I have found a pretty root digger."

"Get rid of them," his father said. "That is not a root digger, and that is not a dog."

"But I want a root digger," the woman said. "And let our son have the little dog."

"Let it be so," the man sighed. "But if we have trouble, remember that you brought it upon yourself and our son."

The woman and her son went to pick berries while the man went hunting for a buffalo. He killed a buffalo cow, threw the bones and skin into the stream, and brought the meat to the lodge. When the woman and son returned, she roasted some of the meat. While they were eating the meat, the little boy fed the dog three times. When he offered more to the dog, his father took away the meat.

As everyone slept that night, Napi and the young man arose, became themselves again, and ate some of the meat.

"You are right," the young man said. "This man is surely the one who has hidden the animals."

"But we must wait," Napi said. When they had eaten, they again changed into the dog and the root digger.

The next morning, the woman and her son went out to dig roots. She took the root digger with her while the dog followed the little boy.

They passed by a cave. A buffalo cow stood near the opening. The dog ran into the cave and, slipping out of the woman's hand, the root digger followed, slithering over the ground like a snake. They found all the buffalo and other game in this cave. They drove them out, and the prairie was soon covered with buffalo, antelope, and deer.

The man ran up to his wife and son, demanding, "Who is driving out my animals?"

"The dog and root digger are in the cave," the woman answered.

"What did I tell you!" he cried. "See what trouble you have brought upon us."

He slipped an arrow into his bow and waited for them to emerge from the cave. However, as the last large bull was thundering from the cave, the dog and the root digger grasped it by the long hair under its neck. They held on until they were far out on the prairie, then changed back into themselves and drove the buffalo toward their camp.

When the people saw the buffalo, they tried to drive the herd over a cliff known as a *piskun*. But just as the first buffalo were about to jump, a raven descended, flapped its wings, and cawed. The buffalo turned and headed the other way. The people tried again, but every time a group of buffalo was about to plunge over the piskun, the raven frightened them away. Napi then realized that the raven was the man who had hidden the buffalo.

Napi went down to the river and changed into a beaver. He lay on a sandbar, as if dead. The raven, who was very hungry, flew down and began to pick at the beaver. Suddenly, Napi snatched the raven by the legs and ran to the camp where the chiefs gathered to decide what to do with the bird.

"Let us kill it," some argued.

"No, it is better if I punish it," Napi assured them.

He tied the raven over the smoke hole in the lodge. As the day went by, the raven grew thin and weak. Its eyes were blinded by the smoke. The bird cried incessantly for Napi to take pity. One day, Napi untied the raven and ordered it to assume its rightful form. He then told the man, "Why have you tried to fool Napi? Look at me. I cannot die. I made the mountains, and they are standing yet. I made the prairies as you now see them.

"Go home to your wife and son," he said. "And when you need food, hunt like everyone else. If you do not, you will go hungry and die."

That is how the buffalo and other wild game returned to the plains.

As settlers moved west into the Blackfeet territory, they brought Christianity with them. Like most tribes at this time, some of their people converted. The rich tradition of storytelling and the ability of their people to keep their language and traditions alive have created a space where the Blackfeet ceremonies and rituals remain intact today. The stories of survival, depicted in art and song, give present-day Blackfeet a glimpse of what kind of life their ancestors lived hundreds of years ago.

There are still sweat lodges on the **reservations** today, and active shamans that tend to their people. This is perhaps the most holistic practice—caring for the physical and spiritual well-being of their people. Events like the Sun Dance keep these ceremonies relevant, celebrated, and a part of the present day. These celebrations draw visitors as well and expose more people to the ways of the Blackfeet Nation.

Many Blackfeet people endured difficult times in the 1800s and 1900s.

CHAPTER FIVE

OVERCOMING HARDSHIPS

The Blackfeet had survived for hundreds of years on this great plain without interruption from European influence. However, things changed as years progressed. In the nineteenth and twentieth centuries, American settlers arrived, seeking new opportunities in the West. For the Blackfeet, it is one thing to survive a harsh winter and another to survive the onslaught of settlers looking to grab as much land and as many resources as possible, at any cost. The Blackfeet soon learned that another man's word was not currency but only flash paper to gain a foothold in their territory. The trust they knew as family members to each other soon became broken in their dealings with settlers. It was more than enough to kill a person's spirit when seeing their land taken without promised payment. That, followed by watching your men, women, and children dying of smallpox by the dozens, would have completely devastated most. The Blackfeet were not most people.

Adapting to a Changing World

In 1855, the Blackfeet signed their first peace treaty with the United States. This agreement came to be known as Lame Bull's Treaty after the great Piegan chief of the same name. At this time, the Piegan (southernmost of the three Blackfeet tribes) separated into two groups, northern and southern. In exchange for **ceding** a vast stretch of Montana north of the Missouri River, the southern Piegan were granted a hunting ground between the Missouri and Musselshell Rivers. They were promised annual payments for the land they had ceded, but they never received any money. Viewing themselves as British subjects, the northern Piegan refused to deal with the Americans and withdrew into Canadian territory, where they have continued to live. An unratified treaty of 1865 and the Fort Laramie Treaty of 1868 further reduced Blackfeet lands in the United States. Moreover, the Blackfeet in Montana, whose lands had traditionally been north of the Missouri, were now assigned to lands south of that river.

In the 1860s, tensions mounted as settlers pushed into the sprawling grasslands and began to graze their herds of cattle on Blackfeet land. People were further

The People and Culture of the Blackfeet

The lands the Blackfeet called home changed with the arrival of US settlers.

angered when the annual payments promised in Lame Bull's Treaty were not received. In 1865, Blackfeet warriors and ranchers clashed over the use of grazing lands. In 1869, Piegan warriors killed a rancher named Malcolm Clark in retaliation for the murder of Blackfeet member Mountain Chief's brother. That same year, a smallpox epidemic struck the Blackfeet. This was the second such epidemic to strike the tribe, the other having occurred in 1837, and it further weakened the tribe. In 1870, US soldiers mistakenly attacked the camp of Heavy Runner, a peaceful chief, while pursuing Clark's murderers. The troops slaughtered about 200 people, mostly women and children, and captured about 140 more in what came to be known as the **Massacre** on the Marias River. The Blackfeet never again confronted the US Army in battle.

In 1874, the US Congress established the Blackfeet Reservation in Montana—on what was a small portion of their former territory. In each treaty negotiated with the United States, the Blackfeet lost more lands to the United States and Canada. Smallpox epidemics continued to devastate the bands, as did the loss of the buffalo and the widespread use of whiskey. The Blackfeet in Canada fared no better. In 1877, they were forced to sign Treaty Number 7, in which they surrendered much of southern Alberta. In exchange, the Canadian government established small reserves for the Blackfeet.

After the buffalo were hunted to near extinction, the great herds suddenly did not appear on the prairie during the winter of 1883–1884. About six hundred Blackfeet, mostly southern Piegan, starved to death in what came to be known as Starvation Winter. With the loss of the buffalo, the Blackfeet became a sedentary people dependent on government rations. Officials encouraged them to take up farming. However, this experiment failed, and around 1890, the Piegan began to raise livestock on tracts of land assigned them by the Bureau of Indian Affairs. A few Blackfeet prospered, but most leased their land to non-Natives, who frequently did not pay for grazing rights.

In treaties negotiated between 1887 and 1896, the United States seized more Blackfeet lands, and the size of the reservation dwindled. The Treaty of 1896 was forced on the Blackfeet when gold was discovered on Blackfeet land. This land later became part of Glacier National Park. The Blackfeet still dispute the terms of this treaty. In 1907, an amendment to the Dawes Act of 1887 allotted 320 acres (130 hectares) of reservation land to each tribal member. The US government sold the remaining Blackfeet land to Montana homesteaders. By 1920, disease, sickness, and war had reduced the Blackfeet population in Montana to two thousand people. Most of these survivors were impoverished and dependent on the US government for food and supplies. Between 1907 and 1921, they were forced to sell more than 200,000 acres (80,937 ha) of land to escape starvation or to pay back taxes. During this time, the Blackfeet in Canada also lost much of the land on their reserves. In both Canada and the United States, Blackfeet children were taken away from their families and sent to boarding schools operated by missionaries. People moved from tipis into log cabins. More importantly, their entire culture—including the Blackfeet language—was threatened.

People began in the 1920s to raise livestock, operate grain farms, and plant subsistence gardens, all of which helped the Blackfeet survive these desperate years. After the passage of the Indian Reorganization Act of 1934, the Blackfeet in Montana adopted their

A member of the Blackfeet tribe plows a farm, circa 1900.

own constitution. In 1935, the Blackfeet Tribal Business Council was formed to manage the business and administrative affairs of the reservation. The city of Browning, Montana, became the center of economic and government activity on the reservation. Living conditions gradually improved for tribal members. The US government also provided credit to help the Blackfeet expand their cattle ranches, which boosted income for many people. By the end of World War II, nearly one-third of the Blackfeet in the United States had moved off the reservation. By the 1960s, the Blackfeet had become more self-sufficient and able to govern

The People and Culture of the Blackfeet

themselves. Yet, traditions continued to be abandoned, and by the 1970s English had replaced Blackfeet as the language for most people on the reservation.

Language and Learning

The Blackfeet speak a language in the Algonquian family of languages. This group of languages is spoken by many tribes living in the eastern forests and around the Great Lakes, as well as on the western plains. As they migrated west, the Blackfeet encountered Native peoples who spoke Athapascan, Shoshonean, and Siouan languages. Their language was influenced by these languages, especially since they lived apart from other Algonquian-speaking peoples. Although the Blackfeet recorded significant events—wars, treaties, acts of bravery, hunting incidents—in pictographs on tipis and buffalo robes, they did not have a written language.

The following examples are based on "The Languages of the Plains: Introduction," by Ives Goddard in *The Handbook of North American Indians*, volume 13 (Plains). Data for this article were obtained from the *Blackfoot Dictionary of Stems, Roots, and Affixes* by Donald G. Frantz and Norma Jean Russell. Blackfeet (or "Blackfoot," as linguists usually say) is a complicated language, but the pronunciation key and examples should be helpful for arriving at a basic pronunciation of the words.

Blackfeet vowels are generally pronounced as follows:

a	as in father
á	as in cut

i	as in t*i*n
í	as in mach*i*ne
o	as in g*o*
ó	as in w*o*man

A glottal stop, or small catch in the throat, is the slight pause as in uh-oh! This is indicated by an apostrophe (').

Here are some everyday words used by the Blackfeet.

kiá-yowa	bear
ksísskstakiwa	beaver
sisttksíwa	bird
i-ní-wa	buffalo
ksi-stsikóyi	day
pí-ta-wa	eagle
pakóyittsiyi	fire
moyísi	house
kokótoyi	ice
nína-wa	man
mi-stáki	mountain
ko'kóyi	night
ó-hkotoka	rock
á-pi-kayiwa	skunk
pitsí-ksi-na-wa	snake
ko-na	snow
kakató'siwa	star
na-tó'siwa	sun
pisstá-hka-ni	tobacco
mi-stsísa	tree
aohkí-yi	water

As with most Native American tribes, the history of the tribe is conveyed through the oral tradition. The history and the culture of each tribe is best preserved and handed down by using traditional language. In a society whose main language is English, followed closely by Spanish, all tribes are finding it much more difficult to keep their language arts growing.

Today, efforts are being taken to preserve the Blackfeet language. Initiatives like the Piegan Institute program (http://www.pieganinstitute.org) keep the language and culture a part of everyday life. This program provides an approach that includes social, intellectual, academic, and linguistic facets. It is an immersion technique that takes into account each student's environment.

Language is a living, breathing art form. It needs to be nurtured and kept whole in order to keep it a thriving and vibrant part of our past, present, and future.

This statue stands at the entrance to the Blackfeet Nation today.

CHAPTER SIX

Nowadays we have the freedom to keep on with the modern ways or to live by our traditional ways if we want to. Until recently, our younger generations were not given this choice to make.

—Beverly Hungry Wolf

THE NATION'S PRESENCE NOW

There is a saying that the strongest sword is forged by metal that has been melted by the hottest fire. The Blackfeet Nation faced adversity and near extinction multiple times. Each and every time, they survived and came back stronger than before. In the face of a frozen landscape, disease, famine, and war, they survived. They step into the future with lessons learned from their past and with hope towards their future as an ever-growing tribe. They have still held on to their skills of using their given resources. They are keeping their history alive, as it has carried them this far.

Blackfeet Nation

Today, the Blackfeet live on both sides of the United States and Canadian border—in northwestern Montana and southern Alberta. The Blackfeet in Montana are left with 1.5 million acres (600,000 ha). The Canadian tribes have even smaller holdings on three reserves. In Canada, the Blackfeet Tribe has changed its name to the Siksika Nation, although people there often refer to themselves as the "Blackfoot." The northern Piegan, spelled "Peigan" in Canada, are today known as the Pikani Nation. All three tribes continue to share a common language and similar traditions. In 1780, there may have been about 15,000 Blackfeet, but in 1809, when trader Alexander Henry took a census, there were only 5,200. In the US census of 1880, there were 2,200 Blackfeet. In Starvation Winter, three years later, 600 perished. In the 1910 census, 2,268 Blackfeet were living on the reservation. Nearly destroyed as a people, the Blackfeet are slowly recovering from decades of war, disease, and poverty. There are now over 32,000 Blackfeet in Canada and the United States combined. In Montana, the Blackfeet Tribe has more than 17,300 enrolled members. Many live on the reservation.

In Montana, the Blackfeet Reservation encompasses much of northwestern Montana, including most of Glacier County. Alberta borders it on the north, Glacier National Park on the west, and the Badger–Two

This sketch depicts the Blackfeet Treaty Council of 1855.

Medicine portion of the Lewis and Clark National Forest on the southwest. Other boundaries include Birch Creek and Cut Bank Creek. The land consists of rolling plains, rising westward to the forests of the Continental Divide. Elevations on the reservation range from 3,400 feet (1,036 m) in the southeast to over 9,000 feet (2,743 m) at Chief Mountain on the northwest edge. The majority of the land is owned by the tribe. Many people support themselves through ranching or employment in oil and natural gas industries.

Blackfeet Government

The Blackfeet tribes in the United States and Canada enjoy their own governments. Since the Indian Reorganization Act of 1934, the Montana reservation has been governed by its own bylaws and a body known as the Blackfeet Tribal Business Council. In its complex relationship with the federal government, the reservation is a sovereign nation within the United States, recognized through treaties, executive orders, laws, and other agreements. Council members are popularly elected by the enrolled members of the Blackfeet Indian Nation. Tribal elections for all council seats and officers are held every two years. Tribal executive officers (chair, vice-chair, and secretary) are nominated by the Business Council. The tribe continues to undertake efforts to improve life for its members by providing excellent schools, businesses, and cultural programs.

Living Off the Land

Farming their fertile land, the Blackfeet in Montana produce a variety of crops, including spring and winter wheat, oats, barley, and alfalfa. A little over 20 percent of this land is irrigated. Tribal members also raise a large number of livestock, including cattle, sheep, horses, and a small herd of buffalo. A small portion of the reservation is forested. These forests consist primarily of stands of conifers, lodgepole pine, spruce, Rocky Mountain alpine fir, and Douglas fir. Coal, oil, and natural gas are the three principal mineral resources on the reservation. About 12 miles (19 km) long and 1 mile (1.6 km) wide, the Blackfeet Coalfield has deposits of an estimated 30 to 50 million tons (27 to 45 million metric tons) of bituminous coal. Two oil and gas fields are located partly within the reservation, while a third oil and gas field lies entirely within the reservation. These fields have been actively developed since the

1950s. Other minerals extracted from reservation lands include gold, silver, lead, and zinc.

Each tribe offers the community different services, such as health care, education, and businesses. Services offered on the Siksika Reserve in Canada include health care facilities, schools, Old Sun Community College, and a number of service stations. The Blood Reserve also provides health care, education, economic development, and land management. On the Peigan Reserve, there are counseling services, educational facilities, and ranches. In Montana, the Blackfeet Nation provides opportunities to explore farming, language preservation, and tourism.

The Blackfeet continue to be deeply concerned about their sacred land. Having lost much of their territory, they have spent years claiming disputes to water rights and portions of Glacier National Park and discussing the appropriate use of tribal lands. Attracting millions of visitors each year, the park is the region's primary tourist attraction. It is hoped that a growth in tourism will benefit the Blackfeet—in both Montana and Canada. Park visitors may be attracted to cultural events and shops on the reservation and reserves.

Preserving the Past and Moving Forward

The Blackfeet are also concerned about preserving their language and traditions. Language classes are offered on the Montana reservation and on reserves in Canada. Established in 1976, Blackfeet Community College is located on the reservation in Montana. Bloods in Canada operate Red Crow Community

A Blackfeet woman named Mary Bad Marriage poses with a pouch she won.

The People and Culture of the Blackfeet

College, and a local college offers classes on the Siksika Reserve. The University of Lethbridge has a Native studies program focused on Blackfeet culture. The tribe manages the nationally known Museum of the Plains Indian in Browning, Montana, and several festivals are held on the reservation every year. Held during the second week in July at the Blackfeet Tribal Fairgrounds, North American Indian Days is one of the largest gatherings of Native people on the continent. It includes traditional dances and a rodeo.

In the years since the Blackfeet have become self-governing, they have steadily improved their health care, education, and housing standards. They have also enjoyed greater economic prosperity as ranches have grown; coal, oil, and natural gas reserves have been tapped; and factories and many small businesses have been established. The Blackfeet have also enjoyed a cultural revival as a growing number of people learn to speak the language. Others reverently take part in the Sun Dance or gather for prayers in the sweat lodge. Many people still honor the power of the medicine bundle and guardian spirits. By successfully confronting economic and social challenges, as well as keeping alive the traditions of their ancestors, the Blackfeet may be assured of a promising future for their children and grandchildren.

Very few societies, races, or even religions carry a thread of continuity within their membership. The Blackfeet have never forgotten their beginnings and traditions. The honor of attending the Sun Dance and offering prayers of thanks for their strong ancestors while praying for a bright future is a powerful homage to the Blackfeet's past, present, and future.

CHAPTER SEVEN

It was hard but when it was over, I was proud of myself and all that I accomplished.

—Minnie Spotted Wolf

FACES OF THE BLACKFEET

When reading these short depictions of centuries of lives well lived, it seems so miniscule in comparison to the great things accomplished by each one. The equality of the men and women becomes apparent as you see both strong women and men that played a pivotal role in the tribe's success and, at times, survival. Thankfully, some of the people are still alive today and are helping to raise yet another generation of strong Blackfeet men and women.

Douglas Cardinal's architectual designs are unique.

Douglas Cardinal (1934–), architect, was born in the village of Red Deer in the province of Alberta, Canada. He is the oldest of eight children. In 1953, he enrolled in the School of Architecture at the University of British Columbia. Asked to withdraw from the school because his designs were too original, he completed his education at the University of Texas in 1963.

Upon his return to Canada, he was asked to design a private residence, a round house that became known as the Guloien House in Sylvan Lake, Alberta. He next designed Saint Mary's Roman Catholic Church in Red Deer, Alberta, again in a circular form, which was acclaimed an architectural triumph. Cardinal

The People and Culture of the Blackfeet

quickly achieved a reputation as a highly innovative architect who blends traditional concepts, such as the sacred hoop, with the latest technology, such as computer-enhanced drawings. He designed the Canadian Museum of Civilization in Hull, Quebec, and the campus master plan for the Institute of American Indian Arts in Santa Fe, New Mexico. He was selected as architect for the National Museum of the American Indian in Washington, DC. In this complex assignment, he had to design a building that could house over a million objects, yet fit into the last remaining site on the National Mall. He has six children. He and his wife reside in Aylmer, Canada.

Crowfoot, circa 1885

Crowfoot (Isapo-Muxila) (circa 1825–1890), warrior and chief, was born a Blood near present-day Calgary, Alberta. After his father's death, he moved north to the lodge of his mother's new husband and was raised as a Siksika Blackfoot. He took part in his first battle at age thirteen and became well known as a fierce warrior, especially against the Cree, the traditional enemies of the Blackfeet. In 1866, he earned the respect of settlers when he rescued Albert Lacombe, a Catholic priest, from hostile warriors. In 1870, he rose to become head chief. He advocated having peaceful relations with settlers pushing into his homeland and refused to ally with Sitting Bull and the Oglala Sioux, who had escaped to Canada after the Battle of the Little Bighorn in 1876.

In 1877, because of his great skills as an orator and diplomat, Crowfoot was principal spokesman for the Blackfoot Confederacy in Treaty Number 7, which ceded 50,000 acres (20,234 ha) of land in what is now southern Alberta to Canada. In 1883, Crowfoot worked for peace between Native peoples and the Canadian Pacific Railway, which was laying tracks through the Canadian prairies. The railroad nearly destroyed the hunting grounds of the Blackfeet. Crowfoot was rewarded for his peacekeeping efforts with a pension from the railroad.

In 1885, Crowfoot's adopted son Poundmaker joined an uprising in Canada known as the Second Riel Rebellion. Crowfoot refused to take part in the rebellion and fight settlers encroaching on Blackfeet lands. However, he encouraged his people to help any Cree refugees who were passing through Blackfeet territory. Crowfoot experienced great tragedy when he lost most of his children to smallpox and tuberculosis. In later years, he devoted himself to traveling as a peacemaker among the Blood, Piegan, Sarsi, Gros Ventre, and Assiniboine peoples in Canada and Montana.

James Gladstone (Akay-na-muka or Many Guns) (1887–1971), political leader, was born at Mountain Mill in Alberta. He grew up on the Blood Reserve in Alberta, Canada, where he was known as Akay-na-muka. He attended Calgary Industrial School, after which he worked briefly as a typesetter for the Calgary Herald. In 1911, he became a scout and interpreter for the Royal Northwest Mounted Police. About this time, he married Janie Healy, with whom he had six children.

Gladstone had a ranch to which he brought many innovations. He was the first Native on the reserve to have electricity and use a tractor. He became well known for his agricultural skills in herding cattle and raising crops and readily shared his knowledge with other Blood farmers and ranchers. He worked to improve living conditions and education on the reserve, as well as to preserve traditional culture. He often served as a representative for his people in trips to Ottawa, the capital of Canada. Gladstone became the first Native American to serve as a senator in the Canadian Parliament. He also encouraged Native people to fight for their rights and become more involved in the administration of the reserve. In 1939, he founded the Indian Association of Alberta and served as president from 1948 to 1954 and again in 1956. In 1958, he was named honorary president.

Beverly Hungry Wolf

Beverly Hungry Wolf (1950–), author, was born in Cardston, Alberta, the daughter of Ruth (Beebe) Little Bear and Edward Little Bear. A member of the Blood tribe, she learned English when she attended a boarding school on the reservation. She has long been involved in preserving the traditional culture of the

Blackfeet. In 1971, she married Adolf Hungry Wolf, an author, with whom she had four children. She taught the children at home without a telephone or electricity.

She has enjoyed a varied career as a teacher's aide at Saint Mary's Indian School on the Blood Reserve, mother, housewife, and publisher of a family-owned business known as Good Medicine Books. With her husband, she has written a number of books, including *Blackfoot Craftwork's Book* (1977), *Siksika: A Blackfoot Legacy* (1979), *Pow-wow* (1983), *Shadows of the Buffalo: A Family Odyssey among the Indians* (1983), *Children of the Sun: Stories by and about Indian Kids* (1987), *Indian Tribes of the Northern Rockies* (1987), and *Daughters of the Buffalo Women: Maintaining the Tribal Faith* (1996). She also wrote the critically acclaimed *The Ways of My Grandmothers* (1980).

She lives on an isolated homestead in the British Columbia Rockies but often travels to the reserve to maintain her place within the tribal society.

Mountain Chief (Ninastoko) (1848–1942), chief and research informant, was born in what is now southern Alberta, Canada, along the Old Man River. When he was a young man, Mountain Chief fought neighboring tribes, notably the Crow and Gros Ventre in 1867 and the Kootenai in the following year. In 1873, he was wounded in the leg in a battle against Crow warriors and thereafter walked with a limp. In 1886, he signed a treaty with the US government and ceded Blackfeet territory east of the Sweet Grass Hills in Montana. In 1895, he agreed to another treaty in which the Blackfeet surrendered the land that would become Glacier

National Park. During the early 1920s, Mountain Chief became well known as a prominent leader in Montana. The last hereditary chief among the Blackfeet, he traveled to Washington, DC, several times to meet with presidents and government officials. He also worked as an informant to General Hugh Lenox Scott, who was studying the sign language of the plains tribes.

Natawista (1825–1893), peace negotiator, interpreter, and trader, was born and raised in Blood country in what is now Alberta, Canada. When she was fifteen, Natawista journeyed south with her father to Fort Union, the post established by the American Fur Company in 1829 at the confluence of the Missouri and Yellowstone Rivers. Natawista married Alexander Culbertson, the head of the trading post, in 1840. In the twenty years of their marriage, they had five children.

After the wedding, Natawista settled at Fort Union and occasionally traveled with her husband to the American Fur Company headquarters in Saint Louis. In 1845, the Culbertsons moved up the Missouri River to establish Fort Benton. Natawista earned a reputation as an excellent hostess for visitors to the fort. She also became a peacemaker between non-Natives and the Blood, Siksika, Piegan, and Gros Ventre people who came to the fort. In 1853, when Culbertson was appointed to a Pacific Railroad surveying expedition through Native American territory, Natawista accompanied him and helped to communicate the peaceful nature of the expedition.

The Culbertsons became wealthy through trade and retired to a mansion in Peoria, Illinois. While living there, Natawista became a consultant for anthropologist Lewis Henry Morgan. She explained kinship relations of the Blackfeet and Gros Ventre. Over time, the couple's fortune was exhausted, and they returned up the Missouri River to again earn a living as traders. After moving west, Natawista became disillusioned with her husband and life in non-Native society. She returned to her home and lived with her nephew until her death.

Earl Old Person (Cold Feet, Stu Sapoo, Charging Horse) (1929–), tribal leader, was born in Browning, Montana, the son of Juniper and Molly (Bear Medicine) Old Person, both of whom were prominent and respected leaders in the community. As he grew up on the reservation, he learned many of the traditions of the Blackfeet and performed dances and songs at the lodge at East Glacier and across Montana. He attended grade school at Starr School and graduated from Browning High School. He married Doris Bullshoe, with whom he had six children.

In 1936, Old Person first sang and danced traditional dances and songs at the Montana state high school basketball championship game in Great Falls. Over the years, he made presentations about Blackfeet culture at schools, colleges, and civic organizations throughout the United States. During the 1940s, he worked at the Museum of the Plains Indian in Browning.

In 1954, at age twenty-five, Old Person became the youngest member of the Blackfeet Tribal Business Council, which is the governing body on the reservation. Ten years later, in 1964, he was

Earl Old Person speaks about the tribe in June 2010.

elected chairman of the tribal council. In 1978, he was appointed honorary chief of the Blackfeet Nation for life. Under Old Person's leadership, the Blackfeet have built a community college, community center, and industrial park on the reservation, along with new schools and houses. Old Person has also overseen the establishment of the Museum of the Plains Indian and a tribal buffalo herd on the reservation.

Over the years, Earl Old Person has been actively involved in a number of civic activities for which he has received many awards. He has met and consulted with many national and world leaders and celebrities. In 1957, he attended the inauguration of President

Dwight Eisenhower. In 1972, he was invited by the shah of Iran to attend the 2,500th anniversary of the Persian Empire. In 1978, the queen of England invited him to attend the Commonwealth Games in Alberta, Canada, where he met the royal family. In 1993, he attended the inauguration of President Bill Clinton. He was invited to participate with other tribal leaders in the opening ceremonies of the 2002 Winter Olympics in Salt Lake City, Utah, and in 2007, he was inducted into the Montana Indian Hall of Fame.

Running Eagle (Brown Weasel Woman) (ca. 1820–ca. 1850), warrior, was born in what is now Alberta, Canada. The oldest of five children, she was named Brown Weasel Woman as a girl and later came to be called Running Eagle. When her father, a prominent warrior, taught Running Eagle's brothers how to hunt and wage war, she asked to join the lessons. Despite her mother's objections, Running Eagle was taught by her father and was soon able to kill a buffalo.

On a hunting expedition, Running Eagle, her father, and the others in their party were attacked by enemy warriors. As they fled, her father's horse was shot and Running Eagle bravely rode back in the face of the warriors to rescue him. Afterward, she was honored for her heroic deed. When her mother became ill, Running Eagle cared for her younger siblings. When Running Eagle was still a young woman, her father was killed in battle, and her mother died soon after. Left alone to care for her brothers and sisters, Running Eagle brought a widow into their home to care for the children. With her father's rifle, she then began to live like a man.

Wanting to be a warrior, Running Eagle followed a raiding party to a Crow camp and convinced the leader to allow her to join them. The Blackfeet stole many horses, including the eleven that Running Eagle captured herself. On the way home, Running Eagle was guarding the stolen horses when she spied two Natives trying to steal them. She shot one of the thieves and chased the other away.

Although some Blackfeet praised Running Eagle for her skill and courage, others disapproved of her role as a warrior. Upon the advice of several elders, she went on a vision quest to guide her destiny. She returned after four days and declared that she had received great powers. She was permitted to join a war party and then take part in a medicine lodge ceremony. During this ceremony, she was given the name Running Eagle. In the ensuing years, Running Eagle led many successful raids and war parties. She refused several offers of marriage and died in battle in the mid-1850s.

James Welch (1940–2003), author, was born in Browning, Montana, of a Blackfeet father and a Gros Ventre mother. Growing up in Native American culture, he was immersed in the traditions and religion of the Blackfeet. He attended the University of Montana, where he earned a bachelor's degree. He taught writing and Native studies as an adjunct professor at the University of Montana and at Cornell University.

Beginning in 1974, Welch published four critically acclaimed novels and a book of poetry. In life, he was widely recognized as one of the foremost contemporary Native American authors. Much of his writing focused on the relations between Native American and non-Native cultures, including *Riding the Earthboy 40, Winter in the Blood, The Death of Jim Loney, Fools Crow*, and *The Indian Lawyer*. Welch cowrote the screenplay for *Last Stand at Little Bighorn* with Paul Stekler. The documentary won an Emmy Award and was part of the *American Experience*, shown on PBS. They also cowrote the history *Killing Custer: The Battle of Little Bighorn and the Fate of the Plains Indians* (1994). *Winter in the Blood* (1974) was adapted as a film by the same name and produced by Sherman Alexie in 2012.

Welch was a member of the Board of Directors for the Newberry Library D'Arcy McNickle Center in Chicago. He served on the Parole Board of the Montana Prisons Systems and died at his home in Missoula, Montana, in 2003.

Without each of these prominent Blackfeet, the tribe's story could have ended like many others. The Blackfeet have a quiet strength and perseverance that has carried them far. Their history is full of peacekeepers, warriors, orators, writers, and politicians. They are all leaders, all family members of this Blackfeet tribe. Like a strong tipi, without each of these strong members of the tribe, their structure could have blown away in the wind.

CHRONOLOGY

mid-1500s The Spanish bring horses to the American Southwest.

circa 1730 The Blackfeet see horses for the first time when they are attacked by Shoshone on horseback. They refer to the horses as "elk dogs."

1730–1750 The Blackfeet acquire horses in trade with neighboring tribes, such as the Flathead, Kootenai, and Nez Perce.

1780 Hudson's Bay Company establishes Buckingham House on the Saskatchewan River in Canada, in Blackfeet country. The Blackfeet obtain guns through trade.

1781 A smallpox epidemic sweeps through Blackfeet territory, killing hundreds of people.

1780–1805 The Blackfeet nearly wipe out the Shoshone in battles over hunting territory.

1787 Blackfeet warriors journey south toward Santa Fe, New Mexico, where they steal horses from the Spanish.

1806 Meriwether Lewis, of the Lewis and Clark Expedition, encounters the Blackfeet at the junction of Two Medicine

River and Badger Creek. He notes that the Blackfeet are a strong and honest people.

1809 Trader Alexander Henry undertakes a census indicating a total of 5,200 people in the Piegan, Blackfeet, and Blood tribes.

1830 The Blackfeet population grows to eighteen thousand people.

1831 The Blackfeet and Americans first engage in trade.

1833 Prince Maximilian, a German scientist and explorer, and Karl Bodmer, a Swiss artist, spend a month with the Blackfeet at Fort McKenzie. Bodmer paints portraits of Blackfeet leaders and Maximilian studies the Blackfeet men's societies.

1837 A second smallpox epidemic kills nearly six thousand Blackfeet.

1845–1857 Smallpox epidemics ravage the Blackfeet, reducing the tribe to between five and six thousand people.

1846 Father Pierre-Jean de Smet offers the first Catholic mass among the Blackfeet.

1855 Lame Bull's Treaty is signed, the first peace treaty between the Blackfeet and the United States.

1860 Settlers push into Blackfeet territory and graze herds of cattle on the sprawling grasslands.

1863 Annuity payments from the US government to the Blackfeet do not arrive. The Blackfeet send a letter of protest to Washington, DC.

1865 Fighting breaks out between the Blackfeet and settlers over the use of grazing lands.

1869 Malcolm Clark is killed by Piegan warriors in retaliation for the killing of Mountain Chief's brother. A smallpox epidemic strikes the Blackfeet.

1870 Massacre on the Marias River. US soldiers mistakenly attack the camp of Heavy Runner while pursuing the murderers of Clark. They kill 200 people and take about 140 women and children prisoner.

1872 A school for Blackfeet children is opened at the Teton River Agency.

1873–1874 By executive order, US president Ulysses S. Grant reduces Blackfeet lands that had been guaranteed by the Lame Bull Treaty. The Blackfeet are neither consulted nor compensated for these losses.

1875 Agent John Wood urges the Blackfeet to organize themselves politically. Little Plume is elected head chief. A tribal code is written.

1878 Prairie fires sweep through the grasslands west of Canada's Cypress Hills, driving the buffalo herds south into Montana. They never migrate north again.

1880 US census counts 2,200 Blackfeet.

1882 The Blackfeet have a successful winter buffalo hunt in Montana, with no hint that the buffalo would quickly vanish.

1883–1884 The Blackfeet endure Starvation Winter when the buffalo herds suddenly disappear. Six hundred people starve to death during the winter and spring. The Blackfeet no longer hunt buffalo but become a sedentary people, dependent on government rations.

1889 First group of Blackfeet students are admitted to Carlisle Indian Industrial School in Pennsylvania.

1892 A boarding school for the Blackfeet opens at Willow Creek, west of present-day Browning.

1893 The Great Northern Railroad lays track through Blackfeet territory.

1896 The Blackfeet sell the land that is to become Glacier National Park for $1,500,000, to be paid at $150,000 per year for ten years.

1903 White Calf, the last head chief of the Piegan, dies during a visit to Washington, DC.

1910 US census reports 2,268 Natives living on the Blackfeet reservation, about the same number as in 1880.

1907–1912 US government attempts to do away with

reservations by dividing them into allotments. Blackfeet Reservation land is divided among individuals. Each person receives 320 acres (129 ha), to be held in trust by the government.

1920 Blackfeet cattle herds wiped out by a severe winter. Many people face starvation.

1924 Native Americans, including the Blackfeet, become citizens of the United States.

1934 Congress passes the Indian Reorganization Act, reversing the Curtis Act and allowing Native Americans to establish tribal governments. The Blackfeet Tribal Council is formed.

1941 Museum of the Plains Indian opens in Browning, Montana.

1972 Pencil factory opens on the Blackfeet reservation.

1978 Earl Old Person becomes chief of the Blackfeet Nation.

1979 All Montana public school teachers on or near reservations are required to have knowledge of Native American studies.

1970s–present The Blackfeet turn to their elders to preserve the language, stories, and traditions of their ancestors. North American Indian Days celebration is held annually on the reservation. The Blackfeet tribe is still around today, with over thirty-two thousand members in the Canada and United States combined. They are primarily ranchers and farmers.

1978 Percy DeWolfe elected to State Senate.

1983 Piegan Institute is established in Browning, Montana.

1987 Blackfeet National Bank, the first tribally owned, federally chartered bank on a reservation is established. The American Museum of Natural History returns Blackfeet human remains taken from Old Agency on Badger Creek.

1994 Tribally controlled community colleges received Land Grant Status. Heart Butte High School completed.

2001 15,441 enrolled Blackfeet members.

2005 Charging Home Stampede Park opens in Browning.

2006 Glacier Peaks Casino opens in Browning.

2009 New Browning High School is opened.

GLOSSARY

breechcloth A cloth or skin worn between the legs and around the hips; also breechclout.

buckskin Deer hide softened by a tanning or curing process.

cede To give up or surrender objects, usually land.

Great Plains A vast area of prairie stretching across North America from Texas to Canada.

massacre The slaughter of a large number of people.

medicine bundle A rawhide pouch containing sacred objects, often carried into battle.

missionaries Christians who tried to convert Native Americans to their religion.

moccasins Soft leather shoes often decorated with brightly colored beads.

pemmican Pounded dry meat mixed with fat and berries, used as "energy food" by warriors on long journeys.

quillwork A decorating technique that uses quills as artwork.

reservation A tract of land set aside by the government as a home for a Native American tribe; called a "reserve" in Canada.

scalp The hair and skin from the head of a defeated enemy.

shaman A holy man or woman responsible for the spiritual and physical healing of tribal members.

Sun Dance Sacred ceremony held every summer in which the Blackfeet give thanks for their good fortune.

sweat lodge A dome-shaped hut covered with buffalo skins in which purifications and other sacred ceremonies are held.

talisman An object believed to bring good luck to a person. The Blackfeet obtained their talismans through vision quests.

tipi Cone-shaped home made of poles covered with animal skins.

travois A sled made of two poles lashed together and pulled by a dog or horse.

treaty A signed legal agreement between two nations.

tribal council The legal governing body of the Blackfeet reservation.

vision quest A ritual in which an individual, purified in a sweat bath, goes alone to fast and pray in hopes of receiving a vision from a spirit who would thereafter serve as a personal guardian.

warbonnet A feathered headdress worn by Blackfeet warriors.

BIBLIOGRAPHY

Bastien, Betty. *Blackfoot Ways of Knowing: The Worldview of the Siksikaititapi.* Calgary, Alberta: University of Calgary Press, 2004.

Glenbow Museum. *The Story of the Blackfoot People: Nitsitapiisinni.* Calgary, Alberta: Firefly Books, 2013.

Goble, Paul. *Buffalo Woman.* Scarsdale, NY: Bradbury Press, 1984.

Grinnell, George Bird. *Blackfoot Lodge Tales: The Story of a Prairie People.* Lincoln, NE: University of Nebraska Press, 1962.

Hungry Wolf, Beverly. *The Ways of My Grandmothers.* New York: William Morrow, 1998.

McClintock, Walter. *The Old North Trail; or Life, Legends and Religion of the Blackfeet Indians.* Lincoln, NE: University of Nebraska Press, 1968.

Tatsey, John, and Paul T. DeVore. *The Black Moccasin; Life on the Blackfeet Indian Reservation.* Spokane, WA: Curtis Art Gallery, 1971.

Welch, James. *Fools Crow: A Novel.* New York: Viking, 1986.

Wissler, Clark. *Mythology of the Blackfoot Indians*, second edition. Lincoln, NE: Bison Books, 2008.

FURTHER INFORMATION

Want to know more about the Blackfeet? Check out these websites, videos, and organizations.

Websites

Blackfeet Nation: Montana Governor's Office of Indian Affairs

http://www.tribalnations.mt.gov/blackfeet

This website provides information about the Blackfeet Nation in the United States today.

Blackfoot, or Siksika, Language

http://www.native-languages.org/blackfoot.htm

Learn some of the Blackfeet language at this website.

"Meet the first Native American woman in the US Marine Corps"

http://www.kpax.com/story/31874009/meet-the-first-native-american-woman-in-the-us-marine-corps

This article discusses the legacy of Blackfeet member Minnie Spotted Wolf, the first Native American woman to join the US Marines.

Native American Facts For Kids, Blackfoot

http://www.bigorrin.org/blackfoot_kids.htm

This easy-to-read website discusses Blackfoot culture and history for students.

Videos

Blackfeet Indian Stories

https://youtu.be/rrCFZQxRQq4

This video includes some Blackfeet stories that were passed down through many generations.

Blackfoot Indian Tribe

https://youtu.be/gnd0icvPfy0

This student-made video explains difficult times the Blackfeet faced in the nineteenth and twentieth centuries.

The Blackfoot Nation

https://www.youtube.com/watch?v=icE-xPDDDKM

Explore the Blackfoot Nation in Alberta, Canada, with the Vaga Brothers.

Organizations

Blackfeet Tribal Business Council

PO Box 850

Browning, MT 59417

(406) 338-7521

http://www.blackfeetnation.com/government

Blood Tribe First Nation
PO Box 60
Standoff, Alberta
T0L 1Y0 Canada
(403) 737-3753
http://www.bloodtribe.org

Museum of the Plains Indian
PO Box 410
Browning, MT 59417
(406) 338-2230
http://www.doi.gov/iacb/museum-plains-indian

Pikani Nation
Box 70
Brocket, Alberta
T0K 0H0 Canada
(403) 965-3940
http://www.piikanination.wix.com/piikanination

Siksika First Nation
PO Box 1100
Siksika, Alberta
T0H 3W0 Canada
(403) 734-5100
http://www.siksikanation.com

INDEX

Page numbers in **boldface** are illustrations. Entries in **boldface** are glossary terms.

The People and Culture of the Blackfeet

The People and Culture of the Blackfeet

ABOUT THE AUTHORS

Kris Rickard grew up on the Tuscarora Indian Reservation and is registered as an Oneida on her mother's reservation in Canada as a proud member of the Turtle clan. Her great uncle was Chief Clinton Rickard, founder of the Indian Defense League of America (IDLA). Rickard is a database administrator working on HIV and breast cancer clinical trials, but she does find time to write and edit as well. She lives with her partner in Buffalo, New York.

Raymond Bial has published more than eighty books—most of them photography books—during his career. His photo-essays for children include *Corn Belt Harvest*, *Amish Home*, *Frontier Home*, *The Underground Railroad*, *Portrait of a Farm Family*, *Cajun Home*, and *Where Lincoln Walked*.

As with his other work, Bial's deep feeling for his subjects is evident in both the text and illustrations. He travels to tribal cultural centers, photographing homes, artifacts, and surroundings and learning firsthand about the national lifeways of these peoples.

The emeritus director of a small college library in the Midwest, he lives with his wife and three children in Urbana, Illinois.